bitten.

unpretentious recipes from a food blogger

For Rob and Sophie, my family and friends.
Without all of you food would be a meaningless means to an end.
With you it is the canvas to countless colourful moments around full and happy tables.

Sarah Graham

*Thank you to Linda and her
amazing team from Struik Lifestyle
for believing in me and giving me
such an incredible opportunity.
Thank you to the always-inspiring
Franck Dangereux for your
foreword and encouragement.*

Published in 2012 by Struik Lifestyle
(an imprint of Random House Struik (Pty) Ltd)
Company Reg. No. 1966/003153/07
Wembley Square, First Floor, Solan Road, Gardens, Cape Town, 8001
PO Box 1144, Cape Town, 8000, South Africa

ISBN 978-1-43170-004-2

Publisher: Linda de Villiers
Managing editor: Cecilia Barfield
Editor: Bronwen Leak
Designer: Beverley Dodd
Photographer: Warren Heath
Food stylist: Lisa Clark
Food stylist's assistant: Sarah Dall
Proofreader and indexer: Joy Clack

Reproduction: Hirt & Carter Cape (Pty) Ltd
Printing and binding: 1010 Printing International Ltd, China

www.imagesofafrica.co.za

IMAGES OF AFRICA
PHOTO LIBRARY

Over 40 000 unique African images available to purchase
from our image bank at www.imagesofafrica.co.za

CONTENTS.

FOREWORD.

In this age of information overload, where social networks have made it possible for people to share everything from their most banal happenings to more personal secrets, secrets that were once written in journals and kept under lock and key, the gates have opened for everyone to share their opinions. The bloggers found their voice and, to my surprise, have brought a refreshing and positive outlook on the food and restaurant scene, raving about good things and sharing tips rather than dwelling on negative bad experiences. They talk about *bien vivre* and *bien manger* and great markets.

I met Sarah. She loves to eat, loves to cook, loves to give and loves to write about it.

This is good. When a great cook who is not a professional cook embarks on a food crusade, in doing so she cuts right down to the essential: simple; in the words of Auguste Escoffier, probably his two most famous words, 'faites simple'. The Frenchman intended to say that the avoidance of all unnecessary complications is key to a soul-fulfilling dish, that the overall process of cooking must exude great care and regard to the quality of the materials, but without too much extravagance; great ingredients cooked with love in a simple way so that they taste how they should.

Sarah and I are very much alike in our food philosophies. I love food that is civilized, without being pretentious … that is to say it has natural tastes, smells and textures, and much character … often it looks beautiful too. What is paramount is that it is prepared with respect, savvy and love …

Sarah's fresh approach to cooking shows us that in our kitchens we are not alone, we bring memories, moments, happy and sad and poignant … In this, *Bitten.* allows you to FEEL the procedure of cooking and the pleasure of eating.

This book is about more than just recipes; it's an account of sorts, with heartfelt anecdotes and a certain *je ne sais quoi* that reveals how simple food without pretence is the perfect palette for creating memories with family and friends that last a lifetime.

And just as guests are welcome at my restaurant fresh off the beach, sand between their toes, kids and dogs in tow, Sarah welcomes you to her kitchen table just as you are. Her uncomplicated love for food and her chatty, self-deprecating, unpretentious approach will make you feel like you're spending time with an old friend.

In essence, *Bitten.* is the antithesis to intimidating food; you will enjoy feasting on these down-to-earth, happy-making recipes for feeding people you love.

Franck Dangereux

Franck Dangereux started La Colombe at Constantia Uitsig in 1996, annually voted one of the best restaurants in South Africa over the last six years. In 2006 he made it to 28th on the list of the world's 50 best restaurants. Franck is now chef patron of the renowned Cape Town restaurant The Foodbarn, along with his business partner Pete.

INTRODUCTION.

It all started with a blog. My blog, that is, afoodieliveshere. com. And then a book proposal, which was accepted. And then I wrote the book. Just. Like. That! (Or very obviously not.) And now here we are …

This book is for people who love life, love food, love their friends and love to squeeze the last drop from their time and money. In its pages you'll find a no-mess no-fuss pretentious-less tribute to wholesome and simple comfort food. I think of it as a quirky cross between a food memoir and a cookbook with delicious, un-intimidating recipes.

My mom always says that there are people who eat to live, and people who live to eat … I am delighted to say that I am undoubtedly and shamelessly the latter. I'm also delighted that my dear Mom has so lovingly archived so many of her own recipes over the years, many of which you'll find here. I have spent countless hours in the kitchen indulging this passion, and blogging about it, so this book is an extension of my delight in sharing my discoveries and my conviction that anyone can cook delicious, wholesome food.

And perhaps I'll start with a proviso … I love food. I am not a chef. So please don't hold me accountable for any of your kitchen calamities. Just like I now scorn the chef who published the 'idiot-proof chocolate cake' recipe, because of my shame at having botched it. Totally and utterly.

And then there's Rob.

He's my legendary husband. A regular bloke (well, way above regular in many ways, that's why I married him) in the sense that he loves food, rugby, fishing, beer, wine … all that blokey stuff. And he's my resident taster. He's super fun to feed as he'll honestly try anything. He's also brutally honest about the results of my culinary creations and has his own repertoire of recipes that would blow your socks off.

In our kitchen we are never alone; we have memories, happy and sad. My love for food is inextricably bound to the pleasures of friendship and great company.

Sarah Graham

FELLOW FOODIE BLOGGERS.

Blogging is interactive. Well, mostly. Bloggers are usually interested in other bloggers and we all chat away in the blogosphere of our choice. In this case, it's the ever-growing foodie one. I wouldn't be anywhere without my foodie-blogger friends and gurus, and so I thought it only fitting to showcase a few other South African food-blogging talents here. I've chosen five of my favourite bloggers and have included one recipe from each of them in the book. Without them, I honestly think this book would be two-dimensional.

And so let me introduce you, in no particular order …

SARAH DUFF, VEGGIE DELISH
http://www.veggiedelish.com

"I love food – thinking about it, cooking it, reading about it and photographing it. I'm a pescatarian (I eat fish and dairy, but no meat) but I cook mostly vegetarian food, and that's what my blog is focused on. Although I love spending time in the kitchen, I don't have the patience for time-consuming complicated cooking, so I choose recipes and adapt them to make them as easy and unfussy as possible. I'm always conscious of eating the right things, and I try to make my cooking healthy without sacrificing taste.

I try to buy seasonally as much as possible, because it's better for the environment and the produce is tastier and healthier. The same goes for organic food, where possible (there isn't a huge range in South Africa yet)."

Sarah's day job is working for the South African *Getaway* magazine.

ANDY FENNER, JAMIE WHO
http://aficionado.co.za/jamiewho

"In his short career as a food writer, Andy – writing under the pseudonym of Jamie Who – has been featured in/written for *Men's Health*, *Women's Health*, *Food&Home*, *WINE*, *House&Leisure*, *Eat Out*, and the *Eat Out* and *Eat In* newsletters.

He was recently named one of the '200 Young South Africans you must take for lunch' by the *Mail & Guardian* and he says he is expecting your invitation!

He is a true foodie, with a strong emphasis on ethical farming and eating. He believes people should pay more attention to where the food on their plate comes from, but at the same time believes 'anybody can cook'. As a result, his tone is deliberately laid back and informal."

JANE-ANNE HOBBS-RAYNER, SCRUMPTIOUS
http://whatsforsupper-juno.blogspot.com

"I'm a freelance journalist, editor and author, a cook, food writer and recipe developer, and a mother of three. I've lived in Johannesburg for the past 17 years, and have recently moved, with my family, to Hout Bay, which is about half an hour's drive from the centre of Cape Town, South Africa.

I've been cooking since I was nine or so, but it's only in the last 12 years that cookery has turned from a hobby into something of an obsession. And no, I'm not going to say, like those annoying TV cooks, that I am 'passionate' about food, fresh local ingredients and punchy flavours. (Duh! Doesn't every cook feel that way?) I'm enthusiastic, yes, but I think the word 'passion' should be reserved for activities that involve reading books or removing your knickers.

I can say that I do love food, especially simple home cooking that warms your heart and makes your tastebuds sing. All I want from a plate of food is that it tastes really good, feels lovely on your tongue and fills your stomach with joy."

ALIDA RYDER, SIMPLY DELICIOUS

http://simply-delicious.co.za/

"I am a 24-year-old mother of twins, Aidan and Abigail. They are absolutely the most important little things in my life (after my husband) and without them my life would be a whole lot more boring ... I'm married to my soul mate (yes, I do believe in soul mates), whom I met when I was 17.

Now the part that most of you are interested in. My relationship with food. It started when I was very young, maybe five or six, when I used to BEG my gran to bake cookies with me. My gran was so incredibly patient with me; the kitchen is a magical place where a whole lot can be forgiven. She had the same passion for food as I have. Her whole life was spent either owning a hotel and running the kitchen or running a catering business. Sunday lunches at her house were filled with tables creaking under the immense amount of food piled on top of them and people bustling to get to them. Memories that I will ALWAYS savour."

Voted Best South African Food & Wine Blog 2010 and Best South African New Food Blog 2010.

NINA TIMM, MY EASY COOKING

http://www.my-easy-cooking.com

"Growing up as a country girl in a huge Afrikaner family, my passion for food is so deeply rooted, that it has become an all-consuming hobby/career. To socialise with friends and family without good food being part of the celebration is almost unthinkable. I grew up with wholesome food with tons of flavour and to this day bland food will not be honoured with a place on my plate."

Nina has been a featured publisher on Foodbuzz and her website has been referred to in the Woolworths *TASTE* magazine. Nina has also been nominated twice for the South African Food Blogger of the Year award. She was a guest speaker at the first South African Food Bloggers Conference in 2010 and again in 2011, and was a special guest at the South African Eat In and Eat Out Awards in 2010. Proof of Nina's Cape Town roots is her most-read post for breyani, which had in excess of 27 000 hits over 48 hours.

CONVERSION TABLE

Metric	US cups	Imperial
5 ml	1 tsp	1 tsp
15 ml	1 Tbsp	1 Tbsp
60 ml	4 Tbsp (¼ cup)	2 fl oz
80 ml	⅓ cup	2¾ fl oz
125 ml	½ cup	4½ fl oz
160 ml	⅔ cup	5½ fl oz
200 ml	¾ cup	7 fl oz
250 ml	1 cup	9 fl oz

A FEW TIPS TO SEND YOU ON YOUR MERRY WAY.

KEEP IT TIDY

Clean up as you go along; this means you won't get to the end of the cooking process and your kitchen looks like a bomb went off. I usually keep the bin in the middle of the kitchen floor when I'm cooking, so I can just discard things quickly and easily as I go along.

THINK AHEAD

If we are having people round, I always lay the table before I start cooking; this means that on the odd occasion when you are still enshrouded in steamy kitchen chaos and hear their knock at the door, it still looks like you're ready for them.

WELL-LOVED FOOD

Wherever possible I encourage you to explore where the food you are buying comes from, and to opt for well-loved ingredients.

THINK THIN(NER)

All cottage cheese, cream cheese and yoghurt are fat-free or low-fat unless otherwise stated.

THANK ME LATER

I have thought through each and every recipe included here and given you a 'meals for a month' plan (see page 172). This includes speedy suppers for week nights and lazy weekend food.

'TIL THE LAST BITE

Always make sure you read the recipe the whole way through before you start cooking. I am a classic culprit for always wanting to get right to the good stuff and have learned this the hard way!

GET THE GEAR

Being efficient in the kitchen is a whole world easier when you have what you need at your fingertips – you'll be more likely to cook and you'll save money by not eating out as often. That said, you can improvise in a lot of areas, so don't be put off if you don't have some of these things or can't afford them at this stage. Check out my kitchen and baking starter kits on page 11 for the basics.

BASIC COOKING TERMS.

WHAT IS AL DENTE?

An understanding of this term is vital if you're ever going to have anything to do with pasta, ever. Here's how Adam Roberts, one of my favourite American food bloggers, describes it: 'You want it to be al dente – which means to the tooth. You want to feel the bite, but you don't want it to be raw. Keep tasting and checking and you'll know: when the spaghetti tastes like how you'd want spaghetti to taste – resilient and snappy, not spongy or wormy.' www.amateurgourmet.com

WHAT IS THE DIFFERENCE BETWEEN PUFF PASTRY AND PHYLLO PASTRY?

Puff pastry is a thick, rich, flaky, buttery pastry, the type that croissants are made of. Phyllo pastry, also spelled filo, is tissue-thin pastry dough usually used in a variety of sweet and savoury Greek and Middle Eastern dishes.

WHAT DOES SAUTÉ MEAN?

Ah, zee French! This one means 'fry quickly in a little bit of hot oil'. Oh, and it also means 'to jump'. I guess you could say you make things jump around in the hot pan and oil? Quite a cute picture.

WHAT DOES COULIS MEAN?

The word originates from the French verb meaning 'to strain' and is a form of thick sauce made from puréed and often strained vegetables or fruits. Coulis can be sweet or savoury, for example sweet berry coulis to drizzle over ice cream, mini pavlovas or pancakes.

QUANTITIES OF FRESH VS DRIED HERBS

You'll notice that I use a LOT of fresh herbs in my recipes. That doesn't mean that you need to come undone if you don't have them, you can usually get away by substituting a third of the fresh herbs for dried herbs, as dried herbs usually have a more intense flavour than fresh.

RESTING MEAT

The difference it makes to any meat if you give it a chance to rest for 5–10 minutes, covered loosely with clingfilm or tin foil, is significant. This ensures the meat remains tender, moist and juicy. Also remember it carries on cooking a little after removing from the heat and during resting, so, for example, if you would like your meat medium-rare, take it off slightly sooner and by the time it's finished resting it should be just right.

BASIC BAKING TIPS.

BAKING AT SEA LEVEL

Each and every oven is different, and it takes a little time to get to know yours, as does figuring out your oven's behaviour at sea level. A basic rule of thumb is to add slightly more raising agent and cook on a slightly lower temperature if you are having any issues with basic recipes. All the recipes in this book have been tested at sea level.

GREASING TINS

The easiest method is to take a small square of greaseproof baking paper and a small dollop of butter and work your way around the tin using the paper to hold the butter and smother the surface of the tin gently. I also regularly use non-stick cooking spray.

WHAT DOES CREAMING BUTTER AND SUGAR MEAN?

This means beating them together in a mixing bowl with an electric hand or stand mixer, adding in the sugar a little at a time until well blended, fluffy, smooth and creamy.

BASIC BUTTER-CREAM ICING

This can be easily made using a ratio of about 3:1 of sifted icing sugar to butter, for example 1 cup icing sugar to ⅓ cup butter. Blend by adding about 1 Tbsp hot water and flavour as you like with vanilla essence, lemon juice and zest, etc.

WHAT DOES WHISKING MEAN?

Whisking is used to blend ingredients together or to incorporate air into a mixture using a whisk – a cooking utensil with a narrow handle and a series of wire loops joined at the end.

WHAT ON EARTH IS BLIND BAKING?

Blind baking means baking a pie or tart crust without the filling so that it firms up and doesn't go soggy when you add the filling. As pastry usually shrinks when blind baking, be generous with your pastry, and then either prick it a good few times with a fork before baking or line with baking paper and a layer of lentils or small pebbles to prevent shrinkage. I usually go for the fork method.

TYPES OF FLOUR

Cake flour is the same as regular flour. For cake flour to have the same raising capacity as self-raising, add 1 tsp baking powder to every 100 g cake flour. Self-raising flour has extra raising agents included already.

CAKE TESTING

A cake is usually done when you insert a skewer or sharp knife into the middle and it comes out clean, or if you gently push the top with your finger and it 'pops' back out.

KITCHEN STARTER KIT.

This section is a little companion of convenience as you learn to meander your way through all manner of kitchen idiosyncrasies. All of these should be easily available at your local supermarket or homeware stores.

Equipment: hand/stick blender; electric hand or standing beater; round and square baking tins, loaf tin and 12-hole muffin tin; kitchen scale, preferably electric; grater and small fine grater, used for zesting; set of measuring spoons and cups; 1-litre glass microwave-proof measuring jug; rolling pin; pastry brush; whisk; kitchen scissors; assortment of sharp knives, especially paring and carving knives; wire sieve; colander – generally used for draining vegetables and pasta when cooked; good-quality vegetable peeler; good-quality potato masher; array of wooden spoons, spatulas and a good ladle

INGREDIENTS

In your spice cupboard: dried chilli flakes | coriander | cumin | masala | turmeric | curry powder | cinnamon | nutmeg | dried mixed herbs | black peppercorns | coarse salt
Around and about: fresh garlic | fresh ginger | lemons | limes
Oils and sauces: olive oil | sesame oil | thai fish sauce | green curry paste | soy sauce | thai sweet chilli sauce
Vinegars: white and red wine vinegar | balsamic vinegar
In the freezer: Frozen peas | phyllo pastry | puff pastry

BAKING STARTER KIT.

If you'd like to give baking a bash, here are a few things you'll find useful.

Apron: because you just wouldn't be a bona fide cook without one, now would you?!
Flours and whites: self-raising flour | regular all-purpose flour (i.e. cake flour) | baking powder | bicarbonate of soda | gelatine powder | yeast sachets
Sugars: light brown sugar | castor sugar | icing sugar | old-fashioned brown or muscovado sugar
Essences: vanilla essence | almond essence
Dried fruit: cranberries | apricots | raisins
Chocolate: good-quality dark and milk chocolate (2 large slabs of each)
Dairy: eggs | unsalted butter (never cook with margarine; it's just not done) | fat-free plain yoghurt | cream | buttermilk (you can make your own buttermilk by adding 1 Tbsp white vinegar or lemon juice to 1 litre milk and let it stand for 10 minutes) | fat-free cream cheese | fat-free smooth cottage cheese | mascarpone cheese | assorted cheeses
Nuts and seeds: slivered almonds | whole almonds (unsalted) | walnuts (unsalted) | pecan nuts (unsalted) | cashew nuts (unsalted) | poppy seeds | sesame seeds | sunflower seeds | pumpkin seeds
Other: greaseproof baking paper | clingfilm | tin foil | muffin papers | cupcake cases

BRUNCH.

baked 'faux'

FRENCH TOAST.

This is a handy twist on traditional French toast, and you can watch it bake instead of slaving over the stove. You will then have no trouble scoffing the spoils of your un-arduous labour, trust me. If you prefer baking in individual ramekins, just layer the bread roughly.

Serves 4 | Preparation time 10–15 minutes | **Cooking time** 30 minutes

WHAT YOU'LL NEED

½–⅔ loaf sliced bread (I use wholewheat, but white will also do)
3 cups milk
3 eggs
3 Tbsp light brown sugar
1 tsp ground cinnamon + extra for sprinkling
½ tsp salt
1 tsp vanilla essence or extract
¼ cup slivered almonds

WHAT TO DO

1. Generously grease or line a large, shallow ovenproof baking dish (20 x 30 cm) with baking paper and preheat the oven to 200 °C.
2. Cut the crusts off the bread slices and halve each slice diagonally into a triangle.
3. Layer the bread in the dish, left to right and top to bottom, with the base of one triangle just under the point of the one below, so that they are slightly raised at the point.
4. Combine the milk, eggs, sugar, cinnamon, salt and vanilla essence, and pour over the bread. Sprinkle the top with more cinnamon and scatter over the almonds.
5. Bake for 30 minutes, turning over the slices halfway, until fluffy, slightly crispy and golden.
6. Serve with syrup, fresh berries, crème fraîche or mascarpone.

FROZEN FRUIT SKEWERS
with honey yoghurt.

Serves 4 | **Preparation time** 5 minutes

WHAT YOU'LL NEED
1 cup grapes
1 cup cubed watermelon
½ cup halved strawberries
½ cup raspberries
16 bamboo skewers, the thinnest you can find
½ cup plain yoghurt
1 Tbsp honey

WHAT TO DO
1. Skewer the fruit, alternating between the different types. Once each skewer is full, cut it in half with kitchen scissors.
2. Place in a Tupperware container and freeze for a minimum of 1 hour, or even overnight or a couple of days in advance.
3. When ready to serve, mix the yoghurt and honey, and tip into a small dish. Layer the skewers on a serving platter and serve with the honey yoghurt for drizzling over.

GRILLED VANILLA NECTARINES.

Serves 4 | **Preparation time** 5 minutes | **Cooking time** 5–7 minutes

WHAT YOU'LL NEED
4 ripe nectarines
2–3 tsp old-fashioned dark brown sugar
1 tsp vanilla essence
2 Tbsp honey
¼ cup plain yoghurt

WHAT TO DO
1. Preheat the grill to its highest setting.
2. Cut around the nectarines with a knife so that you get two equal halves, and remove the pips.
3. Place the nectarines cut-side up in a baking dish, mix the sugar and vanilla essence together and sprinkle over.
4. Place under the grill for 5–7 minutes until the sugared surface of the nectarine turns a rich golden brown. In the meantime, stir together the honey and yoghurt.
5. Remove the nectarines from the grill and serve smothered in the honeyed yoghurt. Add a sprinkling of muesli or granola if you like.

BAKED BREAKFAST EGGS

with tomato, red pepper, smoked sausage and feta.

From Jane-Anne Hobbs-Rayner's blog, 'Scrumptious'

Serves 6 | **Preparation time** 10–15 minutes | **Cooking time** 35–40 minutes

WHAT YOU'LL NEED

2 Tbsp sunflower oil

2 red onions, peeled and chopped

2 large red bell peppers, deseeded and finely sliced

1 large chorizo sausage or similar, sliced

a large sprig of thyme

a pinch of sea salt flakes

12 large ripe tomatoes, chopped

1 red chilli, deseeded and finely chopped

1 Tbsp balsamic vinegar

3 cloves garlic, finely chopped

1 tsp Tabasco sauce or to taste

2 tsp ground cumin

1 tsp ground coriander

1 Tbsp sweet paprika

freshly ground black pepper to taste

6 eggs

250 g feta cheese or creamy goat's cheese

a handful of chopped fresh coriander or flat-leaf parsley

WHAT TO DO

1. Preheat the oven to 180 ºC.
2. Heat the oil in a large frying pan over a medium heat and fry the onions, red peppers, sausage, thyme and salt for 5 minutes, or until the vegetables are softened, but not browned.
3. Drain off any excess fat, and then add the tomatoes, chilli and vinegar. Turn up the heat and cook, uncovered, at a brisk bubble for 10 minutes, or until the tomatoes begin to collapse.
4. Now add the garlic, Tabasco, cumin, ground coriander and paprika. Season with plenty of freshly ground black pepper and more salt if necessary. Cover the pan and turn down the heat to its lowest level. Gently simmer for 10 minutes until slightly thickened.
5. Pour the mixture into a large ovenproof dish. If you like, you can use individual dishes. Make six wells in the mixture and break an egg into each. Cover the dish with a lid or tin foil and bake for 10–15 minutes, depending on how you like your eggs done.
6. Break the cheese into dice-sized cubes and arrange around the eggs. Scatter over the coriander or parsley and serve hot with toast or hunks of bread.

really good
GRANOLA.

This granola is great for when you feel the urge to appreciate the simpler things in life. It's sugar-free and packed full of flavour and goodness. I like to think of it as cereal with a halo. Add a couple of grilled nectarines (see page 14) to your bowl, a dollop of natural Greek yoghurt and a drizzle of honey and you'll have a pretty shiny start to the day indeed.

Makes 12 servings | **Preparation time** 5 minutes | **Baking time** 35–40 minutes

WHAT YOU'LL NEED

roughly 2 cups oats
3 Tbsp each of sesame and sunflower seeds
1 tsp ground cinnamon
½ tsp vanilla essence
¾ cup apple juice
¼ cup honey
¼ cup shredded coconut
1 cup chopped raw almonds or pistachios (or any nuts of your choice)
1 cup dried cranberries

WHAT TO DO

1. Preheat the oven to 170 °C. Line a baking tray with baking paper.
2. Combine everything except the coconut, nuts and cranberries, and spread out on the baking tray.
3. Bake for 20 minutes, and then give it a stir, checking that the granola is evenly distributed. Return to the oven and bake for a further 15–20 minutes until golden and quite brittle.
4. Remove from the oven and allow to cool before breaking up the granola and adding the coconut, nuts and cranberries.
5. Store in an airtight container for up to two weeks.

MEALIE BREAD.

Serves 4–6 | Preparation time 10 minutes | Baking time 40–50 minutes

WHAT YOU'LL NEED

3 eggs
1 cup cake flour, sifted
1 Tbsp baking powder
1 cup grated cheese
1 onion, peeled and grated or
very finely chopped
a generous pinch of salt and
freshly ground black pepper
1 x 410 g can whole kernel corn

WHAT TO DO

1. Preheat the oven to 180 °C and line a loaf tin with baking paper.
2. Mix all the ingredients in a bowl, pour into the loaf tin and bake for 40–50 minutes until the loaf is golden and a sharp knife inserted in the centre comes out clean.
3. Serve with bacon and maple syrup or as is with cold butter.

SMOKED SALMON AND SCRAMBLED EGG WRAPS
with Gruyère.

Serves 4 | **Preparation time** 10 minutes | **Cooking time** 10 minutes

WHAT YOU'LL NEED

6 large eggs

6 Tbsp milk

1 Tbsp butter

a generous pinch of salt and freshly ground black pepper

2 Tbsp chopped fresh parsley

4 large flour tortillas

⅔ cup grated Gruyère cheese (or any cheese you prefer)

½ cup roughly chopped smoked salmon

2 Tbsp chopped red onion

4 toothpicks

WHAT TO DO

1. Mix the eggs, milk, butter, salt and pepper in a frying pan over a medium-high heat. Stir continuously, preferably with a heatproof spatula, until you have light, fluffy scrambled eggs. Stir in the parsley, and then remove the eggs from the heat and set aside.

2. Microwave the tortillas for 40 seconds on High and lay each one on a plate.

3. Divide the scrambled eggs, cheese, salmon and onion between the tortillas, layering the ingredients in the middle of each.

4. Fold each tortilla into triangles and secure with a toothpick.

5. Serve with avocado salsa (see page 50) and sweet chilli sauce on the side.

Note: You could easily use bacon instead of smoked salmon.

GAN-NAN'S SWEETCORN FRITTERS
from the farm.

These. Are. My. Very. Favourite. Breakfast. Anythings.

When I was still at school and living at home, hardly a weekend went by that I didn't demand Mom whip up a batch of these for Sunday breakfast. They originate with Mom's Mom on their farm in the Drakensberg, and always evoke memories of that big-sky farm feeling you get out there. Plus, they're a one-dish doddle to make.

Makes 16 | **Preparation time** 5 minutes | **Cooking time** 10 minutes

WHAT YOU'LL NEED

1 x 410 g can cream-style sweetcorn

1 egg

2 Tbsp cake flour

a pinch of salt

2 rounded tsp baking powder

2 Tbsp milk

3 Tbsp vegetable oil

WHAT TO DO

1. Mix all the ingredients, except the oil, in a bowl until you have something resembling the consistency of thick porridge.
2. Heat the oil in a frying pan and scoop heaped tablespoons of the mixture into the pan, leaving about 1 cm in-between each one.
3. Turn them over when bubbles start to appear on the surface of each fritter and they are golden brown underneath (2–3 minutes). Cook for a further 2 minutes on the other side, remove from the pan and set aside on a plate lined with paper towels to drain any excess oil.
4. Continue until you have used all the mixture and serve as soon as possible, or keep them warm and covered in a warming drawer until you are ready to eat.
5. Serve with a good old English breakfast, or slivers of smoked salmon and a dollop of cream cheese.

Camping-proof
BANANA PANCAKES.

We were visiting Kenya and the Maasai Mara for work, and exploring the opportunity of building a tented safari camp in a conservancy bordering the reserve. My dad, Rob and I were led by two of the most intrepid travellers you could hope to meet – Sean and Tesni – and their seven-month-old daughter, Talia, who stole our hearts with her pluckiness. She remained unfazed by endless game-drive hours spent in her car chair, bumpy roads, camping, roaring lions, even poised and powerful Maasai peddling their wares at the car window every now and then. One day, after a glorious early morning game drive, at the end of a long and bumpy road, lay brunch. Now this is what I call cooking with gas …

Serves 4 | **Preparation time** 5 minutes | **Cooking time** 10 minutes | **Rob's rating** 7/10 (He would like to add that this is on the Bush-rating scale, different to the Home-cooking scale of course.)

WHAT YOU'LL NEED

225 g cake flour, sifted
1 Tbsp baking powder
a pinch of salt
1 tsp sugar
2 large eggs, beaten
2 Tbsp melted butter, cooled
1 cup milk
1 Kenyan-sized banana or 2 regular bananas, peeled and roughly chopped
extra butter for frying
optional: 250 g pkt bacon to serve on the side (Not really optional is it?)
syrup to serve (maple is best, but in the bush anything will do)

WHAT TO DO

1. Combine the dry ingredients, preferably in a jug for easy pouring into the frying pan.
2. Add the eggs, butter and milk in stages, mixing well each time. Add the banana and mix in gently.
3. Heat a large frying pan and add about 1 tsp butter.
4. Pour in enough batter to cover the base of the pan if you'd like extra-large pancakes that you can then cut into portions. Alternatively, pour in small dollops of batter for smaller pancakes. You'll know they are ready to flip when you see gentle bubbles form on the surface of the pancakes; then turn and give it about 1 minute on the other side. Continue until you have used all the batter, adding a little more butter to the pan each time.
5. Fry the bacon in a separate pan, and serve with the hot pancakes drizzled with syrup.

Note: If you do take this recipe camping, get really bush-wise and premix the dry ingredients before leaving home so that you then just need to add the eggs, melted butter, milk and bananas before cooking.

BANANA AND PECAN NUT MUFFINS.

Makes 12 | **Preparation time** 10 minutes | **Baking time** 20 minutes

WHAT YOU'LL NEED

3 large bananas, mashed

¾ cup old-fashioned dark brown sugar

1 tsp ground cinnamon

½ tsp ground ginger

½ cup chopped pecan nuts

1 egg, slightly beaten

80 ml melted butter

1 tsp bicarbonate of soda

1 tsp baking powder

½ tsp salt

1½ cups cake flour, sifted

WHAT TO DO

1. Preheat the oven to 180 °C. Grease a 12-hole muffin tin or line each hole with a paper case.
2. Combine the bananas, sugar, spices, nuts and egg, and add the melted butter. Fold in the dry ingredients.
3. Pour the batter into the muffin tin and bake for 20 minutes.
4. Serve with ricotta cheese and berry coulis.

Note: Bananas can be bought in large quantities and frozen in small batches for future use.

AFTERNOON TEA.

PECAN NUT CHOCOLATE BROWNIES.

Makes 16 | **Preparation time** 5 minutes | **Baking time** 35–40 minutes

WHAT YOU'LL NEED

250 g butter
400 g castor sugar
½ Tbsp vanilla essence
4 eggs
125 g cake flour
90 g cocoa powder
½ tsp baking powder
½ tsp salt
120 g chopped pecan nuts or walnuts

WHAT TO DO

1. Preheat the oven to 180 °C. Grease a medium-sized square baking tin or line with baking paper.
2. In a small saucepan over a medium heat, melt the butter and then add it to a bowl with the castor sugar and vanilla essence.
3. Add the eggs, one at a time, beating well after each addition. Sift in the flour, cocoa powder and baking powder, and gently fold in the salt and nuts.
4. Spoon the mixture into the baking tin and bake for 35–40 minutes. The brownies should be dark brown on the outside but still nicely gooey inside.
5. Allow to cool in the tin, cut into squares and serve with a dusting of icing sugar. Store in an airtight container for up to four days.

Note: These freeze really well for up to two months. Simply thaw and microwave before serving. You can turn them into a delicious chocolate dessert by pouring over a rich chocolate sauce.

ROSEMARY BISCUITS.

Makes 30 | **Preparation time** 5 minutes | **Baking time** 15 minutes

WHAT YOU'LL NEED

120 g butter
¼ cup sugar
1 cup cake flour, sifted
1 Tbsp finely chopped fresh rosemary
1–2 Tbsp cold water

WHAT TO DO

1. Preheat the oven to 180 °C and line a baking tray with baking paper.
2. Cream the butter and sugar, and then mix in the flour and rosemary.
3. Add the water and knead the mixture into a manageable dough.
4. Break off bits of dough and form them into teaspoon-sized balls. Place on the lined baking tray.
5. Press down on each ball with the tines of a fork that you have first buttered and then dipped in brown sugar (optional).
6. Bake for about 15 minutes until lightly golden.

Note: Make lavender biscuits using fresh lavender stalks instead of rosemary, or halve the mixture and make half rosemary and half lavender.

EASIEST-EVER DROP SCONES.

Makes 15 | **Preparation time** 15 minutes | **Baking time** 15–20 minutes | **Rob's rating** 7.5/10

WHAT YOU'LL NEED

325 g cake flour, sifted

100 g sugar

1 Tbsp baking powder

½ tsp salt

85 g unsalted butter

1½ Tbsp lemon zest

1¼ cups stoned cherries or berries

1 large egg

1 large egg yolk

1 cup plain yoghurt

WHAT TO DO

1. Preheat the oven to 180 °C and line a baking tray with baking paper.
2. Mix the flour, sugar, baking powder, salt, butter and lemon zest until the mixture has a soft, breadcrumb-like consistency.
3. Add the cherries or berries.
4. In a separate bowl, lightly beat the egg and extra yolk and stir in the yoghurt. Add this to the flour mixture and stir until just combined – be careful not to over-mix.
5. Using two tablespoons, 'drop' dollops of the mixture onto the baking paper, spaced about 2 cm apart, filling the tray with neat rows.
6. Bake for 15–20 minutes.
7. Serve fresh from the oven with jam and whipped cream.

Note: If you are using frozen berries, thaw them first and then drain off the juice.

LEMON AND POPPY SEED CAKE.

Welcome to a light-hearted, sunny twist on the voluptuous anti-depressant that we all know and love.
Welcome, in effect, to Cake Heaven.

Serves 6–8 | **Preparation time** 10 minutes | **Baking time** 35–40 minutes | **Rob's rating** 8.5/10

WHAT YOU'LL NEED

125 g unsalted butter
2 tsp lemon zest
2 tsp lime zest (if you don't have, just use extra lemon zest)
250 g castor sugar
3 eggs
200 g self-raising flour, sifted
1 Tbsp poppy seeds
100 ml plain yoghurt

Syrup

3 Tbsp lime juice
3 Tbsp lemon juice
3 Tbsp castor sugar

WHAT TO DO

1. Preheat the oven to 180 °C. Grease a loaf tin and dust lightly with flour to make absolutely sure the cake won't stick.
2. Mix the butter and zests, and gradually add the castor sugar until the mixture is thick and creamy, beating for 3–4 minutes.
3. Beat in the eggs, one at a time, and then fold in the flour, poppy seeds and yoghurt, alternately, a spoonful at a time.
4. Pour the batter into the loaf tin and bake for 35–40 minutes until golden and a sharp knife inserted into the centre comes out clean. Remove from the oven, prick holes in the top and allow to cool for a few minutes while you make the syrup.
5. To make the syrup, simmer the ingredients in a small saucepan until the sugar has dissolved, and then bring to the boil for 3 minutes without stirring. Pour over the cooled cake and serve.

SIX-MINUTE CHOCOLATE CAKE.

I know this seems like cheating because a) it's a microwave cake and therefore just not quite proper somehow and b) it traditionally comes in the style of an unsophisticated ring cake (which screams microwave), but this is one of those real gems that you are definitely going to thank me for. Like the cheese muffins on page 35, this can be on your plate in 20 minutes, with the majority of that time being lent to foot-tapping while you wait for it to cool just enough to ice. A lot of people are put off by microwave cakes because they think they're dry or stodgy. Not true of this little poppet.

Serves 6 | **Preparation time** 5 minutes | **Baking time** 6 minutes | **Rob's rating** 8/10

WHAT YOU'LL NEED

1 cup cake flour, sifted
1 cup sugar
1 level Tbsp baking powder
3 level Tbsp cocoa powder
a pinch of salt
2 eggs
1 Tbsp cooking oil
1 tsp vanilla essence
1 cup boiling water

Icing

500 g icing sugar, sifted
100 g butter
3 Tbsp cocoa powder
1–2 Tbsp hot water

WHAT TO DO

1. Grease a microwave cake ring (or a round or heart-shaped microwave cake dish).
2. Mix the dry ingredients in a large mixing bowl.
3. In a separate bowl, whisk the eggs, oil and vanilla essence, and slowly add the boiling water, mixing as you pour it in. Add this mixture to the dry ingredients and mix gently to combine.
4. Pour into the cake ring and microwave on High for 6 minutes. Allow to cool while you make the icing.
5. To make the icing, mix the ingredients until smooth, altering the quantities to suit your preferred consistency.
6. Ice the cake and serve as soon as possible.

CARROT LOAF

with coconut cream icing.

Serves 6–8 | **Preparation time** 10 minutes | **Baking time** 40–45 minutes

---

WHAT YOU'LL NEED

230 g (roughly 2 heaped cups)
self-raising flour
2 tsp baking powder
140 g (about ¾ cup) soft light brown sugar
85 g (about ⅔ cup) walnuts or
pecan nuts, chopped
230 g carrots, peeled and coarsely grated
170 g unpeeled apples, cored and
coarsely grated
2 tsp grated fresh ginger, skin left on
1 tsp ground cinnamon
½ tsp ground nutmeg
1 tsp vanilla essence
2 eggs
150 ml oil

Icing

100 g icing sugar
3 Tbsp fat-free or low-fat cream cheese
2 Tbsp coconut cream
1 Tbsp desiccated coconut
1 heaped Tbsp orange zest
1 Tbsp lemon or lime juice

WHAT TO DO

1. Preheat the oven to 180 °C and line a loaf tin with baking paper.
2. Sift the flour and baking powder into a bowl, and then stir in the sugar, nuts, carrots, apples, ginger, cinnamon, nutmeg and vanilla essence.
3. In a separate bowl, whisk the eggs and oil, and then add to the carrot mixture.
4. Pour the mixture into the loaf tin and bake for 40–45 minutes. Turn out onto a wire rack to cool while you make the icing.
5. To make the icing, beat the ingredients together and refrigerate until the cake has cooled. When completely cool, ice generously and serve.

MOM'S CHEESE MUFFINS.

This is Rob's favourite afternoon snack. They're a triple bonus, because they can literally be on your plate oozing melted butter in exactly 20 minutes, your kitchen won't look like a bomb hit it afterwards and you will have only one dish to wash. So, in effect, these muffins are just one more reason to love Mom.

Makes 10 | **Preparation time** 5 minutes | **Baking time** 15 minutes | **Rob's rating** 8/10

WHAT YOU'LL NEED

1 cup cake flour, sifted
1 cup grated cheese
½ tsp salt
½ Tbsp baking powder
½ tsp mustard
a few chopped spring onions or ½ red onion, peeled and chopped
1 cup milk

WHAT TO DO

1. Preheat the oven to 200 °C and grease a muffin tin.
2. Combine the flour, cheese, salt, baking powder, mustard and onions in a bowl, and then add the milk, mixing everything together gently.
3. Spoon into the muffin tin and bake for 15 minutes until golden and puffy.
4. Remove from the tin and allow to cool slightly before serving with cold butter.

Note: Try making these with different kinds of cheeses, including blue cheese and feta.

CHAI TEA CUPCAKES
with orange cream icing.

Since moving to Cape Town, I've struggled to get the simplest cupcake recipe to work. I like to think it has something to do with being at sea level. Either way, I am over the moon that I got my hands on my sister-in-law Justy's recipe, which works perfectly no matter where you are!

Makes 12 large | **Preparation time** 10 minutes | **Baking time** 25 minutes

WHAT YOU'LL NEED

275 g cake flour
1 Tbsp baking powder
120 ml milk
1 tsp vanilla essence
2 chai teabags (leave out for plain vanilla cupcakes)
110 g butter at room temperature
225 g castor sugar
2 large eggs

Icing

3 Tbsp butter at room temperature
9 Tbsp icing sugar, sifted
2 Tbsp orange juice

WHAT TO DO

1. Preheat the oven to 160 °C (fan oven) or 180 °C (normal oven). Line a muffin tin with appropriate-sized paper cases or just grease well.
2. Sift the flour and baking powder into a bowl.
3. Bring the milk and vanilla essence to a simmer in a small saucepan, add the chai teabags, remove from the heat and set aside to infuse and cool.
4. In a large mixing bowl, cream the butter and castor sugar for 4–5 minutes until pale and smooth. Add the eggs, one at a time, beating in each one for 1–2 minutes.
5. Mix in a third of the flour mixture, then a third of the milk mixture (it must be cool). Continue until all the flour and milk have been added, and then mix for a further 1 minute. The trick is to NOT over-mix.
6. Carefully spoon the mixture into the paper cases, filling them to about two-thirds full.
7. Bake for 25 minutes until slightly raised and golden brown. To check that they are cooked, insert a skewer into the middle of the cupcakes. It should come out clean. Remove the tin from the oven and allow to cool for 10 minutes before taking out the cupcakes and placing them on a wire cooling rack.
8. To make the icing, combine all the ingredients until smooth. Ice the cupcakes when completely cool.

NIBBLES.

COURGETTE AND MINT MINI QUICHES.

The mint in these little quiches really makes the flavours pop. They are easy to make in advance and freeze really well, going straight from freezer to oven for hassle-free entertaining. A whole quiche served with a side salad makes the perfect summer lunch.

Serves 6 as a snack or 4 as a starter | **Preparation time** 15 minutes | **Baking time** 12–15 minutes

WHAT YOU'LL NEED

1 x 400 g roll readymade shortcrust pastry, thawed
2 Tbsp olive oil
1 medium onion, peeled and finely chopped
2 cloves garlic, finely chopped
1 cup grated fresh courgettes (baby marrows)
2 Tbsp finely chopped fresh mint
4 large eggs
1 cup milk
a pinch of salt and freshly ground black pepper
2 x 100 g rolls goat's cheese

WHAT TO DO

1. Preheat the oven to 180 °C. Grease a muffin tin or a medium-sized ovenproof pie dish.
2. Roll out the shortcrust pastry and cut circles to fit into the muffin holes. I find it easiest to use a large mug to cut the circles. Once cut, roll them out a bit more and then fit them into the muffin tin. Prick the pastry bottoms a few times with a fork and blind bake for 5 minutes. If you are doing a whole quiche, roll out the pastry to fit the dish, prick with a fork and blind bake for 8–10 minutes or until golden.
3. Heat the olive oil in a frying pan and fry the onion and garlic for 3–4 minutes until soft. Add the courgettes and mint and fry for a further 2–3 minutes. Remove from the heat, pour the mixture into a colander or sieve and let the juices drain off for a few minutes.
4. In a bowl, beat the eggs, milk, salt and pepper, and then crumble in the cheese and add in the courgette mixture. Spoon into the pastry cases.
5. Bake for 12–15 minutes (or 20 minutes for a large quiche) until the egg mixture is set and a light golden brown.
6. Allow the mini quiches to cool before removing them from the muffin tin.

Note: Play around with fillings: try roasted butternut, bacon, leeks, etc.

CROWD-FAVOURITE CHEESE AND TOMATO TART

with basil cream sauce.

Serves 6 as a snack or 4 as a light meal | **Preparation time** 10 minutes | **Baking time** 15–20 minutes

WHAT YOU'LL NEED

1 Tbsp butter
1 medium red onion, peeled and chopped
1 tsp sugar
1 x 400 g roll readymade puff pastry, thawed
1 Tbsp milk
1 cup grated cheese (you can use a mix of cheeses, e.g. Cheddar and feta or goat's cheese)
2 cups grape-sized rosa tomatoes, halved
salt and freshly ground black pepper to taste
½ cup roughly chopped fresh rocket

Basil cream sauce
2 tsp basil pesto
½ cup smooth cottage cheese

WHAT TO DO

1. Preheat the oven to 180 °C. Line a baking tray with baking paper.
2. Melt the butter in a frying pan over a medium-high heat and fry the onion for 5 minutes until translucent. Add the sugar and fry for a further 5 minutes over a low heat until the onion starts to caramelise and turn a light golden brown. Set aside.
3. Roll out the pastry, use it to line the baking tray and lightly brush with the milk. Pressing down with a fork, make a 1 cm border around the edge of the pastry. Although not essential, this will give you a nice neat border.
4. Evenly scatter the caramelised onion, cheese and tomatoes over the pastry.
5. Bake for 15–20 minutes until the pastry is lightly golden.
6. In the meantime, make the basil cream sauce by mixing together the ingredients.
7. Remove the tart from the oven, add a pinch of salt and pepper, and scatter over the rocket. Serve immediately with the basil cream sauce on the side.

Note: The variations are endless: try making this with roasted butternut, blue cheese, courgettes, bacon – all together or separately, as you wish.

ROASTED ASPARAGUS, GOAT'S CHEESE AND PARMA HAM TARTLETS.

Serves 4 | **Preparation time** 10 minutes | **Baking time** 12–15 minutes

WHAT YOU'LL NEED

3 Tbsp butter

4 sheets phyllo pastry

2 x 100 g rolls goat's cheese

12 asparagus spears, lightly steamed

juice of ½ lemon

12 strips Parma ham (or smoked salmon if you prefer)

olive oil for drizzling

salt and freshly ground black pepper to taste

WHAT TO DO

1. Preheat the oven to 200 °C. Line a baking tray with baking paper.
2. Melt the butter in the microwave (about 30 seconds) and then brush each sheet of pastry before folding in half and then in half again to make a four-layered rectangle. Place the rectangles on the tray.
3. Crumble the goat's cheese over the pastry and then add three asparagus spears to each one.
4. Bake for 12–15 minutes until the pastries are golden.
5. Remove from the oven, drizzle each one with a little lemon juice, top with a slice of Parma ham and a drizzle of olive oil, and add a sprinkling of salt and pepper. Serve immediately.

Note: If you are having people round for dinner, you can assemble these pastries completely a couple of hours beforehand, cover and set aside until your guests arrive, then just pop them in the oven and they'll be done in a jiffy.

VERY BELLA BRUSCHETTA
(a.k.a. Posh tomatoes on toast).

Ah, the bounty of summer … These chirpy snacks call for a sunny Saturday afternoon with friends and good wine, but they're just as good any time you can drum up the excuse. Serve as a light alfresco lunch with a side salad.

Serves 4 | **Preparation time** 5 minutes | **Cooking time** 6 minutes

WHAT YOU'LL NEED

4 ripe tomatoes, deseeded and thinly sliced into lengths

1 red onion, peeled and thinly sliced

1 clove garlic, crushed

zest of 1 lemon

juice of ½ lemon

1 Tbsp olive oil

salt and freshly ground black pepper to taste

1 French loaf

extra olive oil for brushing

WHAT TO DO

1. Preheat the oven's grill to its highest setting, and have the top rack in place.
2. In a bowl, toss the tomatoes with the onion, garlic, lemon zest, lemon juice and olive oil. Season with salt and pepper and set aside.
3. Slice the baguette into 2 cm-thick diagonal slices, and brush one side of each slice with olive oil
4. Place the slices on a baking tray, olive oil side down, and grill for about 3 minutes until golden brown. Then turn the slices over and grill for 2–3 minutes before removing from the oven.
5. Place some of the tomato topping on the oiled side of each slice and serve immediately. Alternatively, place the bruschetta on a serving platter with the topping in a bowl for people to serve themselves.

Note: You can add avocado to the above or try one of the following combinations: smoked salmon and cottage cheese with lemon juice and zest; goat's cheese drizzled with pesto; or Camembert and fig. The options are almost endless.

ROASTED BUTTERNUT AND SWEETCORN QUESADILLAS.

Serves 4 | **Preparation time** 10 minutes | **Cooking time** 18 minutes

WHAT YOU'LL NEED

1 cup cubed butternut (you can buy ready-prepared)
½ Tbsp olive oil
salt and freshly ground black pepper to taste
½ cup whole kernel corn
⅔ cup grated cheese, preferably Cheddar or mozzarella
1 level tsp nutmeg
2 flour tortillas

WHAT TO DO

1. Preheat the oven's grill to its highest setting and line a baking tray with baking paper.
2. Microwave the butternut on High in a covered dish for 5 minutes (this will reduce oven cooking time), then spread out on the baking tray and drizzle with the olive oil, and add a pinch of salt and pepper. Stir to coat well. Grill for about 7 minutes until golden, turning halfway through.
3. In a bowl, roughly mash the butternut with the corn, cheese and nutmeg.
4. Spread the filling over one of the tortillas and place the other on top.
5. Place on a baking tray and grill for about 3 minutes on each side, until lightly golden. Cut into quarters or eighths and serve with yoghurt and blue cheese dressing (see page 69), avocado salsa (see page 51) or cottage cheese.

Note: This makes an excellent main meal served with a crunchy side salad.

CREAMY SMOKED SALMON TARTLETS.

Serves 4 | Preparation time 15 minutes | Cooking time 12 minutes

WHAT YOU'LL NEED

1 x 400 g roll readymade puff pastry, thawed

1 Tbsp milk

⅔ cup smoked salmon strips

zest and juice of 1 lemon

2 handfuls watercress, roughly chopped

1 Tbsp horseradish sauce

⅔ cup fat-free smooth cottage or cream cheese

a generous pinch of salt and freshly ground black pepper

WHAT TO DO

1. Preheat the oven to 180 °C. Line a baking tray with baking paper.
2. On a floured surface, roll out the pastry and cut into squares, about 4 x 4 cm. Place the squares on the baking tray, about 5 mm apart, and brush with the milk. Bake for about 12 minutes until lightly golden and fluffy.
3. Meanwhile, mix together the remaining ingredients, keeping aside half of the watercress.
4. Remove the pastry squares from the oven and allow to cool.
5. Shortly before serving, top each square with the salmon mixture, scatter over the reserved watercress and serve.

Note: For a lighter and more posh, though slightly higher-maintenance, version make phyllo pastry shells. Line 12 cupcake moulds or muffin tin holes, each with four 7 x 7 cm squares of phyllo pastry. Brush each square with melted butter before layering them so that the corners of the squares create a petal effect. Bake for about 7 minutes until lightly golden, remove from the oven, cool and then fill and serve as above.

Alternatively, leave the puff pastry intact and serve as a whole 'flatbread' topped with the salmon mixture.

CHICKEN SATAYS.

Serves 4 | Preparation time 5 minutes | Cooking time 20 minutes

WHAT YOU'LL NEED

250 g chicken breast or thigh pieces, cubed

8 bamboo skewers

1 Tbsp olive oil

Satay sauce

1 Tbsp chopped fresh coriander

1 chilli, deseeded and finely chopped

1 clove garlic, finely chopped

2 Tbsp peanut butter

1 Tbsp soy sauce

2 tsp chopped fresh ginger

6 Tbsp coconut milk

zest and juice of 1 lime

1–2 Tbsp honey

WHAT TO DO

1. Preheat the oven to 180 °C.
2. Blend the satay sauce ingredients in a food processor or with a stick blender until smooth.
3. Skewer the chicken cubes onto the bamboo skewers, and then cut each skewer in half so that they are 6–8 cm long. Lay them in a shallow baking dish and pour over the sauce. Drizzle with the olive oil and toss to make sure they are well coated.
4. Bake for 20 minutes until golden, turning halfway through.

Avocado salsa.

SALSAS AND DIPS.

All of these dips are delicious served with toasted ciabatta slices, pita breads or fresh crudités.

AVOCADO SALSA.

Serves 6 | **Preparation time** 7–10 minutes

WHAT YOU'LL NEED

2 ripe avocados, peeled and chopped into roughly
1 cm cubes
½ red onion, peeled and finely chopped
½ red bell pepper, deseeded and finely chopped
1 chilli, deseeded and chopped or
½ tsp dried chilli flakes
2 Tbsp chopped fresh parsley or coriander
juice of 1 lemon
2 Tbsp plain yoghurt or smooth cottage cheese
salt and freshly ground black pepper to taste

WHAT TO DO

Combine all the ingredients and serve with grilled pitas or
tortilla chips.

MANGO SALSA.

Serves 4 | **Preparation time** 5 minutes

WHAT YOU'LL NEED

1 ripe mango, peeled, pitted and diced (about 1½ cups)
½ medium red onion, peeled and finely chopped
1 red chilli, deseeded and finely chopped or
¾ tsp dried chilli flakes
½ cucumber, chopped or 4 mini cucumbers, sliced
½ red bell pepper, deseeded and chopped
3 Tbsp chopped fresh coriander
3 Tbsp fresh lime juice
salt and freshly ground black pepper to taste

WHAT TO DO

Combine all the ingredients in a bowl and serve with
freshly cooked prawns or calamari.

Note: For a variation, add some diced avocado.

DILL CRÈME FRAÎCHE.

Serves 4 | **Preparation time** 5 minutes

WHAT YOU'LL NEED

2 Tbsp chopped fresh dill
½ cup smooth cottage cheese
juice of ½ lemon
a pinch of salt and freshly ground black pepper

WHAT TO DO

Combine all the ingredients and serve with fresh crudités.

ROASTED RED PEPPER, SUN-DRIED TOMATO AND CUMIN DIP.

Serves 4–6 | **Preparation time** 15 minutes

WHAT YOU'LL NEED

2 large red bell peppers, deseeded and roughly chopped
1 Tbsp olive oil
¼ cup sun-dried tomatoes
½ cup hot water
1 clove garlic, chopped
1 red chilli, deseeded and finely chopped or
¾ tsp dried chilli flakes
1 tsp ground cumin
¾ tsp ground coriander
zest and juice of ½ lemon
½ tsp sugar
2 Tbsp smooth cottage cheese
salt and freshly ground black pepper to taste

WHAT TO DO

1. Preheat the oven's grill to its highest setting. Place the chopped red peppers in an ovenproof dish, drizzle over half the olive oil and grill for 8–10 minutes until the skins start to char slightly, but don't burn.
2. Meanwhile, soak the sun-dried tomatoes in the hot water for a few minutes, and then drain.
3. Remove the peppers from the oven and allow to cool.
4. Blend all the ingredients in a food processor until smooth.

SALADS.

GRILLED PEAR AND GOAT'S CHEESE SALAD.

What achievement are you most proud of so far? If I were to answer with my stomach, one might be this exquisitely simple, done-in-ten grilled pear salad that I hope will have you swooning. My head, on the other hand, would say that handing in a cookbook manuscript to a publisher buys a fair amount of toe-curling excitement. And my heart? Well, she would say that little Sophie Grace, our first child who arrived on 20 June 2011 trumps the lot. And while we're talking about hearts, here is some real soul food that you can get excited about as you dash down the supermarket aisles and grab the very few necessary ingredients required to create a happy little salad feast. It's just a little elegant, without being pretentious, and I believe is one of the few salads that can hold its own along with a deep glass of red. Serve with freshly baked ciabatta and add slices of deli-cooked roast chicken for extra oomph if you like.

Serves 4 | Preparation time 10 minutes

WHAT YOU'LL NEED

3 ripe pears, cored and chopped into rough wedges
a little brown sugar for sprinkling
3 cups mixed salad leaves (I like watercress, rocket and baby spinach for this)
½ cup crumbled goat's cheese
⅓ cup roughly chopped pecan nuts
1 Tbsp olive oil
2 Tbsp red wine vinegar or juice of ½ lemon

WHAT TO DO

1. Preheat the oven's grill to its highest setting.
2. Place the pear wedges in an ovenproof baking dish, sprinkle with a little brown sugar and grill for about 5 minutes until golden.
3. Tip the salad leaves onto a serving platter and layer the cooked pears over them. Top with the goat's cheese and pecan nuts, drizzle over the olive oil and red wine vinegar or lemon juice, and serve as soon as possible.

GREEN SALAD
with toasted almonds, asparagus and string beans.

Serves 4 | **Preparation time** 5 minutes | **Cooking time** 5–7 minutes

WHAT YOU'LL NEED
about 20 asparagus spears
about 20 string (green) beans
¼ cup roughly chopped almonds
3 cups mixed salad leaves
1 cup snap peas
2 Tbsp lemon juice
1 Tbsp olive oil

WHAT TO DO
1. In separate pots, cover the asparagus spears and green beans with boiling water and leave to simmer for 5–7 minutes until cooked. Then drain and place them together in a dish filled with cold water. This will stop them cooking and help to keep their nice bright green colour.
2. Meanwhile, toast the almonds in a small frying pan for 5–7 minutes, stirring regularly until they are all a golden brown colour.
3. Place the salad leaves on a platter, and scatter over the asparagus, beans, snap peas and toasted almonds. Drizzle over the lemon juice and olive oil, and serve.

WATERMELON AND FETA SALAD.

Serves 4 | **Preparation time** 5 minutes

WHAT YOU'LL NEED
½ cup rocket, rinsed
2 cups cubed watermelon, pips removed
⅔ cup cubed feta
¼ cup roughly chopped basil
¼ cup roughly chopped mint
2 tsp balsamic reduction or
1 tsp balsamic vinegar
2 tsp lemon juice
a pinch of salt and freshly ground black pepper

WHAT TO DO
1. Scatter the rocket onto a small salad platter and top with the watermelon, feta, basil and mint.
2. Drizzle over the balsamic reduction or vinegar and lemon juice, and sprinkle over the salt and pepper. You're now good to go!

Note: For a variation, add ¼ red onion, finely chopped.

Green salad with toasted almonds, asparagus and string beans.

SPICY MOROCCAN CHICKPEA SALAD.

Serves 4 | Preparation time 10 minutes

WHAT YOU'LL NEED

1 Tbsp olive oil

1 x 400 g can chickpeas, drained and rinsed under cold water

1 clove garlic, chopped

½ tsp dried chilli flakes

3 sticks celery, chopped

½ red bell pepper, deseeded and chopped

1 ripe avocado, peeled and chopped

¼ cup crumbled feta

a handful of chopped fresh mint and parsley or coriander

¼ cup whole kernel corn

zest and juice of 1 lemon or lime

a generous pinch of salt and freshly ground black pepper

WHAT TO DO

1. Heat the olive oil in a saucepan and add the chickpeas, garlic and chilli. Heat through and then remove from the heat and set aside to cool.

2. When cool, place in a serving bowl and add the remaining ingredients. Mix gently before serving.

MEG'S EASTER BARLEY SALAD.

I'm not sure where Meg found this (she's the creative one slash brilliant wedding photographer slash soon-to-be mum), but she brought it round for our Easter Sunday roast lamb dinner, and I've been making versions of it ever since. It goes beautifully with pretty much everything. You can choose to leave out the chilli if you think you can't stand the heat (I won't tell you to get out of the kitchen), BUT, being a little chilli-shy myself, I can honestly say that in this case it adds a delicious kick.

Serves 6 | **Preparation time** 15 minutes | **Cooking time** 30 minutes | **Rob's rating** 'For a salad, this gets 8/10'

WHAT YOU'LL NEED

1 cup pearl barley
3 cups boiling water
1 cup diced butternut (roughly 1 cm cubes)
2 Tbsp butter
1 red onion, peeled and roughly chopped
1 tsp sugar
200 g green beans
⅔ cup cherry or rosa tomatoes
about ⅓ cup roughly chopped mozzarella or feta cheese
1 handful each of roughly chopped fresh mint, coriander, parsley and rocket
3 sticks celery, chopped
2 baby cucumbers or ¼ regular English cucumber, chopped

Dressing
½ cup olive oil
1 chilli, deseeded and chopped
1 large clove garlic, chopped
2 Tbsp honey
½ cup red wine vinegar

WHAT TO DO

1. In a saucepan, gently simmer the barley and boiling water for about 30 minutes until the water has evaporated. Remove from the heat, tip the barley into a colander and rinse under lukewarm water.
2. While the barley is cooking, preheat the oven to 180 °C and roast the butternut in an ovenproof dish for about 20 minutes.
3. On the stovetop, heat the butter in a frying pan and fry the onion for 5 minutes until translucent. Add the sugar and fry for a further 10 minutes until the onion starts to caramelise and take on a golden brown colour.
4. Steam or boil the green beans for 3–4 minutes.
5. To make the dressing, heat the olive oil, chilli and garlic in a saucepan. Remove from the heat and add the honey. When cooled, add the red wine vinegar.
6. Toss all the ingredients together in a large serving bowl and pour over the dressing just before serving.

PIGS ON BOATS

(a.k.a. Parma ham and melon salad).

This is one of Rob's favourite salads, which he smugly christened last year.

Serves 4–6 | **Preparation time** 5 minutes

WHAT YOU'LL NEED

1 ripe melon, cut into 8 wedges
16 slices Parma ham or prosciutto
a handful of fresh rocket leaves, roughly torn
juice of ½ lemon
2 Tbsp olive oil
salt and freshly ground black pepper to taste

WHAT TO DO

1. 'Wrap' each melon wedge with 2 slices of ham and place on a platter.
2. Scatter over the rocket leaves and drizzle over the lemon juice and olive oil before adding a sprinkling of salt and pepper.

WARM BEETROOT SALAD

on fresh greens.

This is a beautiful, comforting winter salad, but don't let the season restrict you – I find that it fits in all year round.

Serves 4 | **Preparation time** 5 minutes | **Cooking time** 12–15 minutes

WHAT YOU'LL NEED

2 large fresh beetroot heads, leaves trimmed and first layer peeled
1 heaped tsp horseradish
1 Tbsp fat-free cream cheese
1 Tbsp fat-free plain yoghurt or cottage cheese
juice of ½ lemon
3 cups mixed salad leaves
1 Tbsp olive oil
a pinch of salt and freshly ground black pepper

WHAT TO DO

1. Roughly chop the beetroot into thumb-sized pieces and boil in salt water for 12–15 minutes until soft when pricked with a fork.
2. Drain the beetroot and coat with the horseradish, cream cheese, yoghurt or cottage cheese and lemon juice.
3. Place the salad leaves on a platter and drizzle with the olive oil. Spoon over the beetroot and the sauce that will have formed, season with salt and pepper, and serve.

STRAWBERRY AND SPINACH LEAF SALAD.

This should really read 'Strawberry, blue cheese, pecan nut, avocado and spinach leaf summer salad', but that was too much of a mouthful – and I'd like to save mouthful allocations for actually eating this thank you. Everything about it is just right: the colours, flavour combinations, textures – it's definitely my new fave. Perfection on a plate.

Serves 4–6 | **Preparation time** 8 minutes | **Rob's rating** 8/10

WHAT YOU'LL NEED

about 3 cups baby spinach leaves
1 cup roughly chopped strawberries
a handful of chopped pecan nuts
½ cup crumbled blue cheese (goat's cheese or feta also works)
1 avocado, peeled and chopped into 1 cm cubes

Dressing

1 Tbsp olive oil
2 Tbsp red wine vinegar
1 tsp brown sugar or honey

WHAT TO DO

1. Gently toss the salad ingredients together in a serving bowl, taking care not to make the cheese or avocado mushy.
2. Mix the dressing ingredients and pour over the salad just before serving.

HEALTHY BABY POTATO SALAD.

I love potato salad, but usually steer clear of swimming-in-mayo versions because they just seem so unhealthy. This option uses lower-GI baby potatoes and fat-free yoghurt as the main ingredients, beautifully dressed up with the zing of mustard and red onions.

Serves 4 | Preparation time 5 minutes | Cooking time 12–15 minutes

WHAT YOU'LL NEED

about 500 g baby potatoes
½ red onion, peeled and chopped
1 apple, chopped
4 sticks celery, chopped
½ cup fat-free plain yoghurt
1 Tbsp Dijon mustard
2 Tbsp chopped fresh parsley
1 Tbsp chopped fresh mint
zest and juice of ½ lemon
salt and freshly ground black pepper to taste

WHAT TO DO

1. Boil the potatoes for 12–15 minutes until soft but not mushy. Drain and tip into a salad bowl.
2. Add the remaining ingredients and stir gently, being careful not to break up the potatoes too much.

Note: For a variation, add bacon and use 2 Tbsp crumbled blue cheese mixed in with the yoghurt instead of mustard.

FRESH CAPRESE SALAD STACKS.

Serves 4 | Preparation time 7–10 minutes

WHAT YOU'LL NEED

3–4 ripe tomatoes, sliced into 5 mm slices

2–3 Tbsp olive oil

zest of 1 lemon

salt and freshly ground black pepper

1 ripe avocado, peeled and sliced into eighths

juice of 1 lemon

1 x 300 g roll mozzarella, sliced into roughly 0.75 cm slices

1 cup basil leaves

8 toothpicks

WHAT TO DO

1. Place the tomato slices on a plate and drizzle with ½ Tbsp olive oil, the lemon zest and a good sprinkling of salt and pepper.

2. Place the avocado slices on another plate and drizzle with ½ Tbsp olive oil, half the lemon juice and a good sprinkling of salt and pepper.

3. Assemble the salad stacks as follows: 1 slice mozzarella, 1 slice tomato, 1 slice avocado, another slice tomato and 1 basil leaf, and 'skewer' with a toothpick to ensure the stack stays intact. Make more stacks until you have used up all the ingredients.

Watercress pesto.

SALAD DRESSINGS.

BASIL OIL.
WHAT YOU'LL NEED

1 heaped cup chopped fresh basil
5 Tbsp olive oil
1 Tbsp lemon juice
a pinch of salt and freshly ground
    black pepper

WHAT TO DO

Blend all the ingredients well.

Note: Add ½ cup plain yoghurt to make
a delicious basil-yoghurt dipping
sauce or dressing.

RASPBERRY VINAIGRETTE.
WHAT YOU'LL NEED

½ cup crushed raspberries
6 Tbsp red wine vinegar
1 clove garlic, crushed
juice of ½ lemon
3 Tbsp olive oil
½ tsp sugar

WHAT TO DO

Blend all the ingredients well.

EASY MUSTARD VINAIGRETTE.
WHAT YOU'LL NEED

1 tsp Dijon mustard
juice of ½ lemon
a pinch of salt and freshly ground
    black pepper
1 Tbsp olive oil

WHAT TO DO

Whisk the mustard and lemon
juice together until creamy.
Add the remaining ingredients
and blend well.

CHILLI-MINT DRESSING.
WHAT YOU'LL NEED

2 chillies, deseeded and chopped or
    1 tsp dried chilli flakes
¼ cup olive oil
3 Tbsp chopped fresh mint
zest and juice of 1 lemon
salt and freshly ground black pepper
    to taste

WHAT TO DO

Blend all the ingredients well.

YOGHURT AND BLUE CHEESE DRESSING.
WHAT YOU'LL NEED

150 g fat-free plain yoghurt
50 g blue cheese
2 cloves garlic, crushed
1 Tbsp olive oil

WHAT TO DO

Blend all the ingredients well.

WATERCRESS PESTO.
WHAT YOU'LL NEED

50 g watercress, rinsed and thicker
    stalks removed
2 Tbsp pine nuts
3 Tbsp olive oil
juice of 1 lemon
1 clove garlic, crushed

WHAT TO DO

Blend all the ingredients together for
2–3 minutes.

SOUPS.

SWEET POTATO AND COCONUT SOUP.

Serves 4 | **Preparation time** 10 minutes | **Cooking time** 30–35 minutes

WHAT YOU'LL NEED

1.5 kg sweet potatoes, peeled and roughly chopped
2 Tbsp olive oil
1 onion, peeled and roughly chopped
1 Tbsp grated fresh ginger
3 Tbsp Thai red curry paste
1 x 400 ml can coconut milk
850 ml vegetable stock
1 Tbsp lemon juice
salt and freshly ground black pepper to taste
2 Tbsp roughly chopped fresh coriander

WHAT TO DO

1. Preheat the oven to 200 °C.
2. Place the sweet potatoes in an ovenproof dish and drizzle with half of the olive oil, then roast for 25–30 minutes until golden and easily pierced with a knife.
3. Meanwhile, heat the remaining oil in a pot and gently fry the onion and ginger for 8–10 minutes until the onion just begins to turn light golden and caramelise. Stir in the curry paste, simmer for 1 minute and then add the roasted sweet potatoes, coconut milk (reserving 2–3 Tbsp in the can) and stock. Bring to a simmer and cook for a further 5 minutes.
4. Remove from the heat, allow to cool and then blend to the desired consistency. Add the lemon juice, season with salt and pepper and reheat. Serve drizzled with the reserved coconut milk and scattered with the fresh coriander.

CARROT AND CORIANDER SOUP.

Soup is as old as food itself. Advancements in science have enabled soups to take many forms … portable, canned, dehydrated, microwave-ready. 'Pocket soup' was carried by colonial travellers, as it could be easily reconstituted with a little hot water. Canned and dehydrated soups were available in the 19th century, supplying the military, covered wagon trains and home pantries.

A few minutes on Google showed me that there is an entire labyrinth of 'the origin of soup' stories out there, from the Byzantine Empire (I have no idea either) to Constantinople. Whodathunkit? That something so simple and rustic has such a colourful tale of evolution. Perhaps you don't give a toss about trivia, suit yourself. My point (pinky promise I do have one) is that whatever the context or inspiration, a pot of soup is a gorgeous blank canvas one can approach with reckless abandon for delicious creativity and anything-goes flamboyance. What's not to love about that? And, another pinky promise, there's a lot to love about this concoction below. The earthiness of the ground coriander blends beautifully with the carrot and sweet potato mix, leaving you warm and fuzzy in your tummy.

As for the fresh coriander, you might be one of those whose nose wrinkles at the mere thought. I used to be. 'It's an acquired taste,' they said. 'It tastes like stink bugs smell,' I thought, 'and while we're at it, telling me it's an acqulred taste is patronizing; surely it implies that I'll like it when my taste buds eventually grow up?' Hmph. Well, guess what? A couple of years and a few meals where for the sake of decorum it was unavoidable later, 1 x taste of fresh coriander eventually acquired. Just don't tell them I told you.

Serve this with toasted crusty bread spread with goat's cheese or a sliver of Parmesan.

Serves 4 | Preparation time 5 minutes | Cooking time 20 minutes

---

WHAT YOU'LL NEED

1 Tbsp vegetable oil
1 onion, peeled and chopped
1 tsp ground coriander
2 tsp chopped fresh ginger
1 medium potato, peeled and chopped
450 g carrots, peeled and chopped
4 cups vegetable or chicken stock
a handful of fresh coriander, roughly chopped
zest of 1 orange
juice of ½ orange
a generous pinch of salt and
freshly ground black pepper

WHAT TO DO

1. Heat the oil in a large pot and fry the onion for 5 minutes until softened.
2. Stir in the ground coriander, ginger and potato, and cook for a further 2 minutes.
3. Add the carrots and stock, bring to the boil, and then reduce the heat. Cover and cook for 20 minutes until the carrots are tender.
4. Remove from the heat and allow to cool slightly before blending with the fresh coriander, orange zest, orange juice, salt and pepper.
5. Reheat in the pot before serving and adjust seasoning to taste.

GEM SQUASH AND LEEK SOUP.

Gem squash have always been one of my favourite vegetables. I've been making this soup since I was at university and Mom sent me packing with the recipe.

Serves 4 | **Preparation time** 15 minutes | **Cooking time** 10 minutes

WHAT YOU'LL NEED

6 gem squash, halved
2 Tbsp olive oil
1 large onion, peeled and chopped
2 cups chopped leeks (5 mm rounds)
2 cloves garlic, roughly chopped
1 tsp dried thyme or 3–4 sprigs fresh thyme, chopped
1 cup milk
2 cups chicken stock
salt and freshly ground black pepper to taste

WHAT TO DO

1. Place the gem squash in a large pot and cover them with water. Boil for 15 minutes or until the flesh is soft. Drain, allow to cool and then remove the seeds using a spoon. Scoop out the flesh and set aside.
2. While the gem squash are cooking, heat the olive oil in a pot and fry the onion, leeks, garlic and thyme. When cooked, add the gem squash flesh to the pot and stir.
3. Add the milk and stock, season with salt and pepper, and simmer for 10 minutes.
4. Remove from the heat and allow to cool to room temperature before blending to the desired consistency, then reheat to serve. Alternatively, serve it chunky, as is. We like to eat this with toasted bruschetta or French loaf topped with goat's cheese and a drizzle of olive oil.

PEA, COURGETTE AND MINT SOUP.

*I love this soup. It's fresh, funky and can be on the table in 20 minutes. I know it sounds very loudly green,
but once you get past that you'll discover something absolutely delicious.*

Serves 4 | **Preparation time** 5 minutes | **Cooking time** 15 minutes

WHAT YOU'LL NEED

1 Tbsp olive oil
1 onion, peeled and chopped
1 medium sweet potato, peeled and diced
(you can use regular potatoes if preferred)
1 clove garlic, finely chopped
6 medium courgettes (baby marrows),
roughly chopped
800 ml vegetable or chicken stock
3 cups frozen peas
¼ cup chopped fresh mint
2 Tbsp fresh lemon or lime juice
½ cup fat-free plain yoghurt
a generous pinch of salt, freshly ground black
pepper and sugar

WHAT TO DO

1. Heat the olive oil in a large pot, add the onion, potato, garlic and
   courgettes and fry for 2–3 minutes.
2. Add the stock, bring to the boil and then turn down the heat and
   simmer for 10 minutes until the potato is soft.
3. Add the peas and simmer for 3 minutes, then remove from the heat.
   Stir in the mint, lemon or lime juice and most of the yoghurt. Allow to
   cool for a few minutes and then blend, adding salt, pepper and sugar
   to taste.
4. Reheat to serve or eat cold as an alfresco option. Garnish with
   a dollop of the remaining yoghurt, a few whole peas and a little
   chopped mint, and serve with toasted ciabatta or baguette slices
   topped with goat's cheese or Parmesan shavings and a drizzle of
   olive oil.

SPICY BUTTERNUT AND CHICKPEA SOUP.

From Sarah Duff's blog, 'Veggie Delish'

Serves 4 | **Preparation time** 10 minutes | **Cooking time** 20–30 minutes

WHAT YOU'LL NEED

1 Tbsp olive oil

1 onion, peeled and roughly chopped

1 heaped tsp harissa paste

1 heaped tsp crushed garlic

1 tsp crushed fresh ginger

½ tsp each of turmeric, cumin seeds and ground cinnamon

5 medium carrots, peeled and roughly chopped

1 kg butternut, peeled and chopped

1 x 410 g can chopped peeled tomatoes

1½ cups vegetable stock

½ cup red lentils, rinsed well

1 x 400 g can chickpeas, drained

½ tsp dried chilli flakes

a small handful of chopped fresh coriander

a small handful of crumbled feta

WHAT TO DO

1. Heat the oil in a medium-sized pot over a medium-high heat and fry the onion for 3–5 minutes until it starts to soften. Add the harissa paste, garlic, ginger, turmeric, cumin seeds and cinnamon, and fry for 2–3 minutes until the spices become fragrant.

2. Add the carrots, butternut, tomatoes and stock. Turn up the heat and let the soup boil for about 10 minutes, and then add the lentils. Continue cooking for about 10 minutes, stirring occasionally.

3. Once the butternut starts to soften, roughly mash it and stir it into the soup. The soup is ready when the butternut has blended well with the rest of the ingredients.

4. Add the chickpeas and chilli, stirring to heat through.

5. Sprinkle individual servings with the coriander and feta.

Note: If you don't have harissa paste, use 1 Tbsp tomato paste mixed with 1 tsp dried chilli flakes.

CHICKEN.

CREAMY DIJON CHICKEN.

From Alida Ryder's blog, 'Simply Delicious'

Serves 4 | **Preparation time** 5 minutes | **Cooking time** 20 minutes

WHAT YOU'LL NEED

2 Tbsp olive oil

4 large deboned skinless chicken breasts (left whole, cubed or flattened)

2 large leeks, finely sliced

2 cloves garlic, crushed

1 cup cream

2 tsp Dijon mustard

1 tsp wholegrain mustard

juice of ½ lemon

salt and freshly ground black pepper to taste

chopped fresh parsley to serve

WHAT TO DO

1. Heat the oil in a large frying pan and fry the chicken until cooked through and browned. Remove from the pan and set aside.

2. In the same pan, fry the leeks and garlic for about 5 minutes until fragrant and softened.

3. Add the cream, mustards and lemon juice, and allow to simmer and reduce for 3 minutes.

4. Return the chicken to the pan, season to taste and mix around to ensure the chicken is well coated in the sauce and heated through.

5. Sprinkle with chopped fresh parsley and serve with a starch of your choice.

Note: Substitute half the cream for plain yoghurt for a slightly more calorie-friendly option.

LAVENDER, LEMON AND THYME ROAST CHICKEN.

Back to Zimbabwe and a farm herb garden for this one. My sister-in-law Justy and I were determined to figure out a recipe right after she came up with the idea. So after some trial and error on both sides of the border, we now have ourselves a new firm favourite Roast Chicken Dinner.

Serves 4 | Preparation time 20 minutes | **Cooking time** 1 hour

WHAT YOU'LL NEED

2 Tbsp butter

2 Tbsp rinsed and finely chopped fresh lavender leaves (not the flowers)

2 Tbsp rinsed and finely chopped fresh thyme leaves (stems removed)

½ tsp each of salt and freshly ground black pepper

1 whole free-range chicken, rinsed and patted dry with paper towels

2 lemons, halved

1 Tbsp olive oil

1 onion, peeled and chopped

about 6 cloves garlic, chopped

about 200 ml good-quality white wine

½ cup chicken stock

1 tsp cornflour (optional)

⅓ cup water

WHAT TO DO

1. Preheat the oven to 200 °C.
2. Mix the butter with the herbs, salt and pepper.
3. Reserving 2 tsp of the mixture, use your fingers to stuff the rest of the herb butter in between the skin of the chicken and the breast meat. Repeat on the reverse side of the chicken, also under the skin, and in the areas where the drumsticks join the body.
4. Place a lemon half, the reserved herb butter, and a few more whole fresh herb leaves (if you have) in the cavity, followed by another lemon half.
5. Place the chicken in an ovenproof dish, drizzle with the olive oil, season with salt and pepper, add in the onion, garlic and the two remaining lemon halves and pour in half the wine. Cover with a lid or tin foil and cook for 45 minutes.
6. After 45 minutes, pour the juices from the cooking chicken into a small saucepan, and then return the chicken to the oven, uncovered. Cook for a further 10–15 minutes until the skin is golden and crispy.
7. Add the remainder of the wine and the chicken stock to the saucepan, and leave to simmer for about 10 minutes until it starts to thicken. Mix the cornflour and water in a jug, and add to the pan to make a lovely thick gravy.
8. Serve the chicken with baby potatoes, fresh green beans and roast onions, with the gravy on the side.

CHICKEN, BUTTERNUT AND FETA PIE.

Serves 4 | **Preparation time** 15 minutes | **Baking time** 25 minutes | **Rob's rating** 8/10

WHAT YOU'LL NEED

1½ cups peeled and cubed butternut (about 1 cm in size)

1 medium red onion, peeled and chopped

1 Tbsp butter

1 tsp sugar

⅓ cup crumbled feta

⅓ cup grated cheese

2 Tbsp cottage cheese

1 cup chopped cooked chicken breast

1 Tbsp chopped fresh sage or 1 tsp dried

1 x 400 g roll readymade puff pastry, thawed

1 egg, beaten

WHAT TO DO

1. Microwave the butternut on High in a covered dish for 5–6 minutes until soft.

2. In the meantime, fry the onion in the butter and sprinkle over the sugar. Cook for about 15 minutes until glazed and golden brown.

3. Preheat the oven to 180 °C and grease a shallow casserole or pie dish.

4. Combine the caramelised onion, butternut, cheeses, chicken and sage in a mixing bowl, and set aside.

5. Roll out the pastry and cut in half. Use one half to line the greased dish.

6. Spoon the mixture into the centre of the dish and spread it out, leaving 1–2 cm around the edge of the pastry.

7. Cover with the second sheet of pastry, trimming it to fit. Press down the edges with a fork and brush lightly with the beaten egg to give the pastry a golden finish.

8. Bake for about 25 minutes until golden. Serve with mashed potato and a side salad.

Note: Try different fillings: leftover roast chicken and roast veggies, bacon and mushrooms, just about anything will work. You can also make mini pies and freeze them for lunchbox snacks or for those days when you just can't face the kitchen.

15-MINUTE LEMON CHICKEN SKEWERS –
because summer says so.

9 November – We're staying in a gorgeous holiday house just south of Cape Town in Simon's Town this month,
complete with breathtaking views over the harbour that just ooze health and happiness. And we're not even on holiday.
(It's a long story that I shan't bore you with, because we have more important things to talk about.) Like these chicken kebabs
that are kind of amazing and just in time for summer – although come to think of it, we all seem to be on time for summer here
in Cape Town this year except for the weather … well tant pis as the French so eloquently say. Never mind! We shall press on as
though summer is indeed in full-fledged perfection, which is exactly how it felt last Tuesday evening when we had these out on our
balcony overlooking the rainbow of little sailing boats.

Serves 2 | **Preparation time** 5 minutes | **Cooking time** 10 minutes

WHAT YOU'LL NEED

250 g skinless, deboned chicken thighs
⅔ cup fat-free plain yoghurt
2 Tbsp olive oil
1 clove garlic, crushed
zest and juice of 1 lemon
1–2 tsp dried chilli flakes or 1 fresh chilli, deseeded and chopped
a handful of chopped fresh basil or coriander
sea salt and freshly ground black pepper to taste
2 kebab skewers, soaked in cold water for 20–30 minutes

WHAT TO DO

1. Put the chicken thighs in a bowl and cover with the yoghurt, olive oil, garlic, lemon zest and juice, chilli and basil or coriander. Add a generous sprinkling of salt and pepper.
2. Leave to rest overnight (if you're organised) or for as long as possible before dinner (if you're like me).
3. Thread the thighs onto the skewers and cook on a preheated Weber or under the oven's grill for 4–5 minutes on each side until slightly charred and tender.
4. Serve with simple summer veggies, a salad or baked potatoes. Enjoy!

Note: You could also do mini versions for tapas or finger snacks.
And try adding wedges of fresh nectarines onto the kebab skewers before cooking.

APPLAUSE FOR PEANUT SESAME CHICKEN.

There was very little conversation at our dinner table. We were both too busy getting acquainted with and wallowing in the glory of this, our NBF. Dead easy. Delicious. Done in 10. What more do you want?!

Serves 4 | **Preparation time** 5 minutes | **Cooking time** 5 minutes | **Rob's rating** 8.5/10

WHAT YOU'LL NEED

3 Tbsp olive oil

4 chicken breasts or 10 chicken thighs, roughly chopped

250–300 g rice or egg noodles

2 cups roughly chopped broccoli

1 red bell pepper, deseeded and chopped

2 Tbsp roughly chopped fresh coriander

1 Tbsp sesame seeds

1 Tbsp toasted flaked almonds (optional)

Sauce

3 Tbsp sesame oil

1 large clove garlic, finely chopped

3 Tbsp soy sauce

6 Tbsp sweet chilli sauce

2 Tbsp smooth peanut butter

juice of 2 limes

WHAT TO DO

1. Heat the olive oil in a wok or pot and brown the chicken pieces until lightly golden on all sides.
2. Meanwhile, in two separate pots, cook the noodles and broccoli for 4–5 minutes. Drain both and set aside.
3. While the chicken, broccoli and noodles are cooking, whisk together the ingredients for the sauce and set aside.
4. Pour the noodles into a warmed serving bowl, add the chicken and broccoli, drizzle with the sauce and then add the red pepper, coriander, sesame seeds and toasted almonds (if using). Serve as soon as possible in warmed bowls.

Note: I recommend only adding the sauce just before serving, otherwise it tends to get absorbed by the noodles and can become a bit dry, and you definitely don't want that – the sauce is too good to waste!

BEAUTIFUL BUTTER CHICKEN BUNNY CHOWS.

Adapted from Jane-Anne Hobbs' blog, 'Scrumptious'

Serves 8 as a snack or 4 as a main meal I **Preparation time** 15 minutes I **Cooking time** 30 minutes I **Rob's rating** 8/10

WHAT YOU'LL NEED

500 g chicken thighs, roughly chopped

½ cup plain yoghurt

2 tsp each of turmeric, medium curry powder, ground coriander, ground cumin and dried chilli flakes (Don't throw all the spices together yet; just keep the boxes out and ready, as you need only half of each to start with.)

2 Tbsp butter

2 Tbsp olive oil

2 cloves garlic, chopped

2 tsp grated fresh ginger

1 tsp freshly ground black pepper

1 x 410 g can chopped peeled tomatoes

2 Tbsp sweet chilli sauce

3 Tbsp ground almonds (the vital secret ingredient!)

12 readymade mini pita breads

100 ml low-fat coconut milk

salt and freshly ground black pepper to taste

a handful of chopped fresh coriander

WHAT TO DO

If possible, the morning before:

Place the chicken in a large bowl and coat with the yoghurt and 1 tsp each of the turmeric, curry powder, coriander, cumin and chilli. Cover with clingfilm and place in the fridge to rest. I have made this without the resting time and it's still delicious; so don't panic if you don't have time.

An hour before serving:

1. Heat the butter and olive oil in a medium-sized pot over a medium-high heat. Add the garlic, grated ginger, black pepper and remaining spices, and let them 'marry' with the oil until fragrant.

2. Add the chicken mix in a couple of batches so that the pot isn't overwhelmed. Stir and let it come to a simmer, 3–5 minutes. Add the tomatoes, sweet chilli sauce and ground almonds.

3. Simmer gently for about 20 minutes. You will know you're close when the colour starts to change to a delicious, rich, burnt orange and the meat is really tender. Try not to stir too often, as this can break up the chicken too much.

4. Heat the oven to 200 °C. Lay the mini pitas on a baking tray, sprinkle lightly with water and bake them for about 1 minute until golden.

5. About 5 minutes before serving, add the coconut milk to the butter chicken and stir gently. Season to taste. Transfer to a serving bowl and sprinkle over the fresh coriander.

6. To serve, arrange the pitas on a platter with the dish of butter chicken and a few teaspoons on the side for serving. Your friends can then spoon the chicken directly into the pitas, making their own 'bunny chows'.

PLUM AND BRIE-STUFFED CHICKEN BREASTS.

I've also made this using cranberries and goat's cheese. You could also use pears, nectarines or figs, and almost any combination of cheeses. Wrapping the chicken in the bacon keeps it deliciously moist. You could also use pancetta or Parma ham.

Serves 4 | **Preparation time** 10 minutes | **Cooking time** 20–25 minutes

WHAT YOU'LL NEED

4 deboned skinless chicken breasts
2 plums, flesh sliced off and roughly chopped
4 slices Brie, each about 5 mm thick
8 toothpicks
8 rashers streaky bacon
olive oil for drizzling
salt and freshly ground black pepper to taste

WHAT TO DO

1. Preheat the oven to 200 °C.
2. Place each chicken breast between two pieces of clingfilm and rest on a chopping board. Using a meat mallet, hammer out the pieces until about 5 mm thick. Remove the clingfilm and spread about 1 Tbsp plum pieces down the middle of each chicken breast, followed by a piece of Brie.
3. Roll up and secure each one with 2 toothpicks. Place two rashers of bacon side by side on a chopping board. Place a chicken breast on the bacon rashers and tightly wrap the bacon around the chicken, attaching them to the toothpicks to further secure them.
4. Place the chicken breasts on a baking tray, drizzle with a little olive oil, sprinkle over some salt and pepper, and cook for 20–25 minutes until the cheese is melted and the chicken is no longer pink in the middle.
5. Serve with mashed sweet potato and a simple green salad on the side.

Note: Reserve the cooking juices and add them to a small saucepan along with another 2 chopped plums. Cook for 5–10 minutes to reduce to a delicious sauce, seasoning with salt to taste.

CHUTNEY CHICKEN CASSEROLE.

As this is my mother-in-law's recipe, I'm obviously rather nervous of getting it wrong, so let me call this a 'loose adaptation' and hope that covers me. It's pretty hard to get wrong though, whatever route you choose to take. Serve this over mashed potato and it's perfection. It's also a really good one if you're cooking for a crowd (just double the quantities) or to make in advance and freeze.

Serves 4 | **Preparation time** 15 minutes | **Cooking time** 45–50 minutes

WHAT YOU'LL NEED

3 Tbsp butter or olive oil

2 medium onions, peeled and chopped

2 cloves garlic, chopped

about 750 g chicken (breasts, thighs or drumsticks, whatever you prefer)

1 x 250 g punnet mushrooms, chopped

1 cup chicken stock

1 cup cream or plain yoghurt

1 cup chutney (Mrs Balls of course)

chopped fresh parsley to serve

WHAT TO DO

1. Heat half the butter or olive oil in a large pot and brown the onions, garlic and chicken pieces.
2. Add the remaining butter or olive oil and the mushrooms, and continue to fry until the mushrooms are browned.
3. Add the chicken stock and bring to a simmer, and then add the cream or yoghurt and chutney.
4. Cook gently for a further 30–40 minutes. Serve over mashed potato or rice with some chopped fresh parsley sprinkled over the top.

two thumbs up for
GREEK LAMB AND FETA BURGERS.

I have been looking for an excuse to try these for ages. This is proper down to earth soul food that you can really sink your teeth into. Yum. This recipe was inspired by my friend Barbs, who I consider a pukka kitchen queen, so you won't be disappointed.

Serves 6 | **Preparation time** 5 minutes | **Refrigeration time** 30 minutes | **Cooking time** 15 minutes | **Rob's rating** 8/10

WHAT YOU'LL NEED

750 g lamb mince
1 red onion, peeled and finely chopped
½ cup crumbled feta
a handful of chopped fresh mint and parsley
(you could also add coriander)
1 tsp ground coriander
1 tsp ground cumin
2 Tbsp lemon juice
1 tsp freshly ground black pepper
1 tsp salt
pita pockets or fresh ciabatta rolls to serve

Tomato relish

½ Tbsp olive oil
1 small onion, peeled and chopped
1 tsp dried chilli flakes
2 cloves garlic, finely chopped
½ tsp ground cumin
½ tsp ground coriander
1 x 410 g can chopped peeled tomatoes
1 tsp sugar

WHAT TO DO

1. Preheat the oven to 180 °C.
2. In a large bowl, mix the mince with the rest of the burger ingredients.
3. Refrigerate for 30 minutes, just so the meat firms up again.
4. In the meantime, make the tomato relish. Heat the olive oil in a small saucepan and fry the onion, chilli, garlic and spices for 2–3 minutes. Add the tomatoes and sugar, and simmer for 10 minutes until it starts to thicken. Tip into a small serving bowl.
5. Roll the mince into patty-sized balls, flatten them slightly between your palms and place them on a platter until the grill is ready – you can either grill these in the oven for 10–15 minutes until just off-pink in the middle, or braai them on a gas Weber.
6. Rest the patties while you toast the pitas or bread rolls for 5 minutes or so.
7. Serve the burgers with sides of the tomato relish, caramelised onions and sweet potato fries. If you are short on time, just use slices of fresh tomato instead of the relish.

OUR ULTIMATE LAMB CURRY.

No repertoire of recipes is complete without the proverbial lamb curry … I do live in the Cape after all, with some of the best Karoo lamb right on our back doorstep. And this one is particularly close to my heart given that it's so easy to throw together and almost never fails to please. What you should try and do is get the lamb marinating in the yoghurt and half the spices the night before or at least the morning before – it takes just 5 minutes to assemble before you fly out the door for work.

Serves 4 | Preparation time 15 minutes **I Cooking time** 1½ hours (Don't worry, it's pretty much a maintenance-free period of cooking.)

WHAT YOU'LL NEED

750 g lamb (I usually go for chump chops and add in a bit of neck for some variety. Almost anything will do though. The key is cooking it for long enough that it goes deliciously tender.)

2 cups plain yoghurt

2 tsp each of turmeric, medium curry powder, ground coriander and ground cumin (Don't throw all the spices together yet; just keep the boxes out and ready, as you need only half of each to start with.)

1 tsp dried chilli flakes

¼ cup olive oil

2–3 cloves garlic, chopped

2 tsp grated fresh ginger

1 tsp freshly ground black pepper

1 x 410 g can chopped peeled tomatoes

2–3 Tbsp chutney

juice of ½ lemon

fresh coriander to garnish

WHAT TO DO
The night/morning before:

Roughly chop the lamb, add it to a large mixing bowl and coat with the yoghurt, half the spices and half the chilli. Cover with clingfilm and refrigerate.

To cook

1. Heat the olive oil in a pot and fry the garlic with the remaining spices and chilli, ginger and black pepper, allowing them to blend with the oil.
2. Add the lamb in a couple of batches so that the pot isn't overwhelmed. Stir and bring to a simmer.
3. Add the tomatoes, chutney and lemon juice and simmer gently for about 1 hour, the longer the better. You will know you're close when the colour starts to change to a delicious, rich, brick-red and the meat is really tender.
4. Garnish with fresh coriander and serve with couscous, basmati rice or naan bread and minted tzatziki on the side.

JAMIE WHO'S SWEET POTATO GNOCCHI
with shredded lamb shank.

From Andy Fenner's blog, 'Jamie Who'

"Gnocchi is highly underrated. It is not overly difficult to make and when you use sweet potato, as I do, it's a lot healthier than most starches. The other bonus is that you can always make extra dough and freeze it. In terms of exact amounts, it's a bit tricky. Just gauge as you go and add flour or water as necessary." – Andy

Serves 4 | **Preparation time** 20 minutes | **Cooking time** 2½ hours

WHAT YOU'LL NEED

4 lamb shanks
flour for dusting the lamb
1–2 Tbsp olive oil
1 onion, peeled and finely chopped
a handful of finely chopped carrot
a handful of finely chopped celery
a handful of hard herbs, chopped (go for thyme, rosemary, origanum or a combo)
3 cloves garlic, crushed
1–2 chillies, finely chopped
2 x 410 g cans chopped peeled tomatoes
about ½ bottle good-quality red wine
a handful of roughly chopped fresh parsley

Gnocchi

3–4 sweet potatoes, peeled, cooked and mashed
about 2 cups cake flour + extra for dusting
1 free-range egg yolk
a pinch of nutmeg
salt and freshly ground black pepper to taste

WHAT TO DO

1. Preheat the oven to 140 °C.
2. Dust the lamb shanks with flour. On the stovetop, heat the olive oil in a deep ovenproof pot and brown the shanks. Remove from the pot and set aside.
3. In the same pot, gently fry the onion, carrot and celery for a few minutes and then add the herbs, garlic and chilli. Fry for a further 2–3 minutes before adding the tomatoes and wine.
4. Return the shanks to the pot. They must be covered in the liquid, so you may need to add a glass or two of water.
5. Bring to the boil before reducing the heat to a simmer. Cook for 10 minutes before placing in the oven.
6. Cook the shanks for at least 2½ hours, but preferably longer, gently turning them every now and then. While the meat is cooking, make the gnocchi (see below).
7. When the meat is falling off the bone, remove from the oven and set aside to cool. Remove the shanks from the pot. Take the meat off the bones and shred.
8. Reduce the remaining sauce in the pot on the stovetop until you have the desired consistency for a nice thick sauce. Return the shredded meat to the pot and heat through.
9. To serve, spoon the lamb and sauce into bowls, top with gnocchi and garnish with chopped fresh parsley.

Gnocchi

1. To make the gnocchi, ensure the sweet potatoes are well mashed and, while still warm, add the flour, egg yolk and nutmeg. Season well with salt and pepper and knead to make a warm, soft dough. If you need to add extra flour or water, do so. Cover with a tea towel and leave to stand for 5 minutes.
2. Roll out the dough on a floured surface to form a long, thin 'sausage'.
3. Using a sharp knife, cut the dough into 1 cm pieces. Using a fork, flatten each piece to form ridges on one side. Place the pieces on a floured baking tray.
4. Bring a pot of salted water to the boil and cook the gnocchi in batches. What's pretty cool is that the gnocchi tell you when they're ready by rising to the surface. When this happens, scoop them out gently with a slotted spoon and set aside in a serving dish for reheating later.

LAMB BOLOGNAISE.

I don't know what it is, but I often find myself turning up the snob factor when it comes to minced meat ... until lately that is. It just didn't seem right to leave it unattended and unloved in my books forever, so I've been giving the not-an-Italian-staple-for-nothing a second chance. Though, if you know me at all by now, you'll know that if I can swap in lamb for anything, I'll do it. So here's to a very simple, but very bella, lamb bolognaise that tastes about 100 per cent better than the sum of its simple parts. Oh, and I can't even claim credit for the recipe; it was my always-smashing, nothing-but-dashing Rob who pulled this together.

Serves 4 | **Preparation time** 5 minutes | **Cooking time** 20 minutes

WHAT YOU'LL NEED

1 x 500 g pkt spaghetti or linguini, whichever you prefer
2 Tbsp olive oil
2 onions, peeled and chopped
2 cloves garlic, chopped
½ tsp each of dried chilli flakes, ground cumin and ground coriander
500 g lamb mince
2 x 410 g cans chopped peeled tomatoes
2 Tbsp tomato purée
2–3 Tbsp chutney
1 tsp salt
2 tsp freshly ground black pepper
chopped fresh parsley and grated cheese to serve

WHAT TO DO

1. Cook the pasta with a dash of olive oil according to the packet instructions. Drain, rinse well under cool water to remove the starch and set aside.
2. Heat the olive oil in a frying pan over a medium-high heat and brown the onions and garlic along with the chilli, cumin and coriander.
3. Add the mince and cook for 2–3 minutes until it has browned.
4. Add the tomatoes, tomato purée, chutney, salt and pepper.
5. Simmer for 15–20 minutes until the sauce takes on a rich, brick-red colour and starts to thicken.
6. Serve over the pasta, garnished with chopped parsley and grated cheese.

Note: If you want to bulk up the dish, or just for a change, add 2 grated medium carrots and 1–2 rashers bacon.

LAMB PITAS

with lemony salsa.

Serves 4 | **Preparation time** 15 minutes | **Cooking time** 20 minutes

WHAT YOU'LL NEED

2 cloves garlic, chopped

3 sprigs fresh rosemary, leaves only

1 tsp fennel seeds

½ tsp salt

2 Tbsp olive oil

about 500 g lamb (I usually use chump chops)

4 large wholewheat pita breads

Lemony salsa

1 ripe tomato, chopped

½ red onion, peeled and finely chopped

⅓ English cucumber, chopped

a handful of fresh mint and parsley, roughly chopped

3 Tbsp plain yoghurt

juice of 1 lemon

salt and freshly ground black pepper to taste

WHAT TO DO

1. Mix the garlic, rosemary leaves, fennel seeds, salt and 1 Tbsp olive oil to make a rough paste. Spoon this mixture over the lamb and leave to rest for a few minutes if you have time.
2. Preheat the oven to 200 °C.
3. Heat the remaining olive oil in a pan on the stove and cook the lamb for 3–4 minutes on each side until just pink in the middle. Cover with clingfilm and rest for 5–10 minutes before slicing into slivers.
4. Mix all the salsa ingredients in a small bowl.
5. Just before serving, bake the pitas in the oven for 3–5 minutes until heated through and golden. Stuff with the lamb and salsa and serve immediately.

RACK OF LAMB
with a couscous and herb crust.

Serves 6 | **Preparation time** 15–20 minutes | **Cooking time** 25 minutes

WHAT YOU'LL NEED
Couscous and herb crust

a large handful of flat-leaf parsley, chopped

2 sprigs fresh thyme, chopped

2 sprigs fresh rosemary, leaves removed from stems and roughly chopped

3 cloves garlic, chopped

1 thumb-size stick fresh ginger, finely chopped with the skin on

zest and juice of 1 lemon

a pinch of salt and freshly ground black pepper

2 handfuls of uncooked couscous

Lamb

2 Tbsp butter

1 Tbsp olive oil

2 racks of lamb

1 sprig fresh rosemary

2 cloves garlic, crushed

2 tsp Dijon mustard

WHAT TO DO

1. Preheat the oven's grill to its highest setting.
2. For the herb crust, blend the herbs, garlic, ginger, lemon zest and lemon juice in a food processor to a pulp. Season with salt and pepper, add the couscous and mix again briefly until blended. Tip the breadcrumb-like mixture onto a plate and set aside.
3. On the stovetop, heat the butter and olive oil in an ovenproof pan over a medium-high heat. Add the lamb along with the rosemary sprig and sear for 2–3 minutes on each side until browned. As it is searing, baste the meat with the pan juices. Add the garlic, cook for a further 2 minutes, then transfer the pan to the oven and roast for 5 minutes.
4. Remove from the oven and set aside somewhere warm to rest for 5 minutes, to let the meat tenderise. Once the lamb has rested, brush it with the Dijon mustard and pat the couscous mixture onto the meaty side.
5. Return to the oven for a further 15–20 minutes (for medium) or until cooked to your liking. Remove from the oven, cover tightly with tin foil and set aside to rest for 3–4 minutes.
6. Carve into individual cutlets and serve on warm plates with garlic and dill mashed potato and minted pea purée (see page 148).

Note: You can also use lamb chops or a lamb roast. Cooking time in the oven will be less with just 1 rack of lamb, probably 10–15 minutes.

LEMON AND ROSEMARY GRILLED LAMB CHOPS

with green pea and mint purée.

Serves 4 | **Preparation time** 10 minutes | **Cooking time** 10–12 minutes

WHAT YOU'LL NEED

zest of 1 lemon

3 sprigs fresh rosemary, leaves removed

½ tsp salt

1 Tbsp butter

4 lamb chops, about 175 g each

Pea and mint purée

1 cup frozen peas, cooked and drained

¼ cup plain yoghurt

¼ cup vegetable stock

1 clove garlic, crushed

2 Tbsp mint leaves

salt and freshly ground black pepper to taste

WHAT TO DO

1. Preheat the oven's grill to its highest setting.
2. In a food processor or pestle and mortar, crush the lemon zest, rosemary leaves and salt together until they start to form a rough paste. Mix in the butter and spread this evenly over the chops before placing them in a shallow ovenproof dish.
3. Grill the chops for 5–6 minutes on each side, leaving them pink in the middle.
4. Meanwhile, to make the purée, blend all the ingredients in a food processor until almost smooth. Serve with the grilled lamb chops and mashed potato or potato wedges.

MUSTARD AND GARLIC ROAST FILLET

with creamy peppercorn sauce.

Serves 4 | **Preparation time** 15 minutes | **Cooking time** 20 minutes

WHAT YOU'LL NEED

750 g beef fillet

3 cloves garlic, cut into thirds

2 Tbsp Dijon mustard

1 Tbsp mustard seeds (optional)

1 Tbsp roughly crushed black peppercorns

a generous pinch of salt

2 Tbsp olive oil

Peppercorn sauce

1 Tbsp black peppercorns

1 Tbsp balsamic vinegar

¼ cup cream

salt to taste

WHAT TO DO

1. Preheat the oven to 220 °C.
2. Pierce the fillet with the tip of a knife making about nine incisions and push a slice of garlic into each one. Mix the mustard, mustard seeds (if using), black pepper, salt and 1 Tbsp olive oil, and spread this over the fillet.
3. Heat a large frying pan on high until very hot and starting to smoke. Add the remaining olive oil and sear the fillet, turning occasionally, for 5 minutes or until brown all over.
4. Transfer the fillet and juices to an ovenproof dish and roast for a further 15 minutes (for medium-rare) or until cooked to your liking. Remove from the heat, cover with tin foil and set aside to rest for at least 10 minutes before carving. This will ensure the meat is as tender as possible.
5. After 10 minutes, pour the juices from the rested fillet back into the frying pan, add the peppercorn sauce ingredients and stir to thicken for 3–5 minutes.
6. Serve the carved fillet with the sauce on the side.

BEEF AND BEER PIE.

Serves 4 | **Preparation time** 5 minutes | **Cooking time** 30 minutes + 15 minutes for the pie

WHAT YOU'LL NEED

500 g cubed beef

salt and freshly ground black pepper to taste

2 Tbsp olive oil

1 level tsp dried thyme or 1 Tbsp chopped fresh

1 medium onion, peeled and chopped

1 large clove garlic, finely chopped

¾ cup beer

1 cup beef or vegetable stock

1 large sweet potato, peeled and roughly chopped

1 cup peeled and roughly chopped carrots

1 Tbsp prepared mustard (I prefer Dijon)

2 Tbsp cornflour mixed with a little cold water

1 x 400 g roll phyllo pastry, thawed

1 egg, beaten

WHAT TO DO

1. Season the beef with salt and pepper. Heat the olive oil in a frying pan over a medium-high heat and cook the beef with the thyme until browned on all sides.

2. Add the onion and garlic, cook for 2–3 minutes, then add the beer and simmer for a further 2–3 minutes.

3. Add the stock, sweet potato and carrots, ensuring they are covered with liquid, and simmer for 20 minutes until the sweet potato is soft. You want the beef to be nice and tender, so do a taste test and if it's still too chewy then continue cooking for a few more minutes.

4. Add the mustard and cornflour, stir until the mixture thickens, season to taste with salt and pepper and then remove from the heat.

5. Preheat the oven to 200 °C and grease a medium-sized ovenproof dish (about 20 x 20 cm).

6. Layer three sheets of phyllo pastry, cut the pile in half with kitchen scissors or a knife and cover with a damp kitchen towel to prevent the pastry from drying out.

7. Spoon the beef mixture into the dish and cover with the sheets of pastry, brushing each one with the beaten egg before adding the next sheet.

8. Bake in the middle of the oven for 15 minutes until the pastry is crispy and golden.

Note: Any cut of beef will do, but the better the cut, the more tender the end result.

BAKED MEATBALLS

with onion and red wine gravy.

From Nina Timm's blog, 'My Easy Cooking'

I think meatballs are seriously underrated. Nina's recipe won't leave you with dried-out meatballs. She serves hers with creamy mashed potato, though you can also serve spaghetti or linguini.

Serves 6 | Preparation time 10 minutes **| Cooking time** 45 minutes

WHAT YOU'LL NEED

4 slices brown bread (not seed loaf)
1 kg beef mince (topside if possible)
1 large onion, peeled and grated or finely chopped
1 Tbsp Worcestershire sauce
2 tsp salt
½ cup chopped fresh parsley (Nina also adds some sage)
½ tsp ground coriander
freshly ground black pepper to taste

Onion and red wine gravy

a little olive oil
3 large onions
1 clove garlic, crushed
½ bottle good-quality red wine
1 cup beef stock
1 sprig of fresh thyme
1 sprig of fresh rosemary
1 sprig of fresh sage, roughly chopped
2 tsp sugar
salt and freshly ground black pepper to taste

WHAT TO DO

1. Soak the bread in water for about 2 minutes. Squeeze to remove all the water and combine with the rest of the ingredients. Mix by hand, but do not over-mix. Shape into small meatballs and set aside.
2. Preheat the oven to 180 °C.
3. To make the gravy, heat a little olive oil in an ovenproof frying pan and fry the onions and garlic until translucent. Add the remaining ingredients and cook until the onions are soft and the sauce has reduced somewhat.
4. Add the meatballs to the sauce and place the pan in the oven for about 45 minutes. The meatballs should be slightly brown on top and the onions reduced to a sticky, intense gravy.
5. Crumble some goat's cheese over the top and serve over creamy mashed potato. It doesn't get better than this!

Note: If you don't have an ovenproof frying pan, use an ordinary pan and then transfer the meatballs and sauce to an ovenproof dish for baking.

BAIE LEKKER BOBOTIE, BOET.

Bobotie is a well-loved South African dish, almost as famous as the 'braai' itself, consisting of spiced minced meat baked with an egg-based topping. It is a dish of some antiquity, with its origins in the Cape of Good Hope dating back to the 17th century, when the Cape Malay community would cook it with mutton. Today it is more likely to be made with beef or lamb.

Serves 6 | **Preparation time** 10 minutes | **Cooking time** 35 minutes

WHAT YOU'LL NEED

2 Tbsp olive oil
2 tsp butter
500 g beef mince
2 medium onions, peeled and chopped
1 clove garlic, chopped
1 apple or carrot, peeled and grated
2 tsp medium curry powder
1 tsp ground coriander
1 tsp turmeric

½ tsp chopped fresh ginger
½ tsp dried mixed herbs
½ tsp ground cinnamon
½ tsp dried red chilli flakes
1 Tbsp chutney
salt and freshly ground black pepper
 to taste
1 Tbsp lemon juice
½ cup seedless raisins
2 Tbsp flaked almonds

2 slices wholewheat bread, soaked in
 water, lightly squeezed and mashed
 with a fork
2 bay or lemon leaves

Custard topping
1 cup milk
½ tsp salt
a pinch of freshly ground black pepper
2 eggs

WHAT TO DO

1. Preheat the oven to 190 °C and grease an ovenproof dish. I use a slightly smaller dish to make a deeper, moister bobotie.
2. Heat the oil and butter in a frying pan and fry the mince, stirring often until loose and crumbly. Add the onions and fry until soft and translucent.
3. Add the garlic, apple or carrot, curry powder, coriander, turmeric, ginger, mixed herbs, cinnamon, chilli and chutney, and cook for 1 minute. Season with salt and pepper. Stir in the lemon juice, raisins, almonds and mashed bread.
4. Tip the mixture into the dish and spread it out evenly. Press the bay or lemon leaves into the mixture.
5. Whisk the milk, salt, pepper and eggs with a fork and pour over the top.
6. Bake uncovered for 30–35 minutes or until the custard topping is firm and golden brown.

PORK FILLET
with rosemary, red onion and pears.

We don't usually eat a lot of pork in our household; I can't think exactly why, but that's just the way it's always been. This really shouldn't be the case though, as it's a generously versatile meat that you can get really creative with. Not to mention it's about half the price of beef.

Serves 4 | **Preparation time** 5 minutes | **Cooking time** 25–30 minutes

WHAT YOU'LL NEED

1 Tbsp olive oil
1 red onion, peeled and roughly chopped
a pinch of sugar
4 x 175 g pork fillets or loin steaks
1 large sprig fresh rosemary, chopped or about 2 tsp dried
3 pears, cored and cut into quarters

WHAT TO DO

1. Heat the oil in a frying pan and fry the onion and sugar for 5–10 minutes or until the onion just starts to caramelise. Remove from the pan and set aside.
2. Add the pork and rosemary to the pan and fry for about 8 minutes on each side, adding a little more oil if necessary, until the steaks are golden and cooked through, showing no pink in the middle.
3. Add the pears and caramelised onion for the final 2 minutes of cooking.
4. Serve with baked potatoes smothered in a creamy mustard sauce made by mixing 1 Tbsp Dijon mustard into ½ cup fat-free smooth cottage or cream cheese.

QUICK CRUSTLESS BACON AND SPINACH TART.

Serves 6 | **Preparation time** 15 minutes | **Baking time** 30 minutes

WHAT YOU'LL NEED

1 Tbsp olive oil

1 onion, peeled and chopped

200 g bacon, chopped (I use kitchen scissors, it's quicker)

175 g fresh spinach, roughly chopped

1 cup grated Cheddar cheese (or any cheese of your preference)

roughly ⅔ cup milk

2 eggs

a pinch of freshly ground black pepper

1 heaped Tbsp cake flour

1 tsp Dijon mustard

WHAT TO DO

1. Preheat the oven to 180 °C and grease a medium-sized pie dish (approximately 20 cm wide).

2. Heat the olive oil in a non-stick frying pan over a medium heat and fry the onion and bacon for 4–5 minutes until the onion has softened and the bacon starts to brown.

3. Remove the pan from the heat and stir in the spinach. Tip this mixture into the pie dish, spreading evenly, and sprinkle over the grated cheese.

4. Beat together the milk, eggs, pepper, flour and mustard and pour over the filling.

5. Bake for 30 minutes or until set and lightly golden. Serve with a light crunchy salad.

Note: Great for a light, speedy supper, this quiche is really versatile: swap the bacon and spinach for chicken and mushrooms or a mix of goat's cheese, feta and blue cheese.

ROAST PORK BELLY

with apricot sauce and apple confit.

Serves 4 | **Preparation time** 10 minutes | **Cooking time** 1½ hours

WHAT YOU'LL NEED

1 kg pork belly, scored diagonally

1 tsp each of salt and freshly ground black pepper

1 red onion, peeled and cut into wedges

2 apples, cored and quartered

1 Tbsp runny honey

2 Tbsp apricot jam

½ Tbsp hot water

1 Tbsp olive oil

1 Tbsp chopped fresh thyme

⅔ cup white wine

WHAT TO DO

1. Preheat the oven to 160 °C.
2. Pour a kettle of boiling water over the pork belly, drain and set aside. This will ensure nice crispy crackling. Rub the salt and pepper into the fat of the belly.
3. Place the pork, onion and apples into a heavy roasting dish.
4. Mix the honey, apricot jam, hot water and olive oil, and drizzle over the pork.
5. Scatter over the thyme and pour in the white wine.
6. Roast for 1½ hours, adding more liquid halfway through if the roasting dish becomes dry.
7. Remove the pork from the dish, cover with foil and rest for 10 minutes before slicing.
8. Carefully pour the apples, onion and cooking juices into a saucepan and simmer for 5 minutes. Mash roughly with a fork, and spoon over the sliced pork to serve.

STICKY PORK BANGERS

with creamy mustard mash.

What's your idea of perfect weather? I find myself in a real quandary when trying to answer that. You have balmy summer evenings when it seems to stay light until midnight, crickets chirping, sun-kissed bare arms and grass-tickled bare feet, ice-cold anything in a glass filled with merrily clinking ice cubes, and so much more. But then, just when you're about to die of an overdose of sublimely summery satisfaction, there is winter. My faithful old friend. He stealthily sneaks in over the hills and, next thing you know, you're socked-up to the nines, sitting by the fire and cracking open another bottle of red after scraping plates clean of the latest comfort food that filled your cosy kitchen with aromas that are so warm and delicious they are almost tangible. Ok, quandary over I guess. You can tell which corner I'd favour if I had to choose. And it's largely because of the food. Such as these yummy, scrummy, plump pork sausages baked in a sticky sauce.

Serves 4 | **Preparation time** 5 minutes | **Cooking time** 25–30 minutes

---

WHAT YOU'LL NEED

8 plump pork sausages
1 Tbsp wholegrain mustard
2 Tbsp clear honey
2 Tbsp chutney
juice of ½ lemon
1 Tbsp olive oil
1 tsp chopped fresh thyme

Gravy

2 tsp gravy powder
¼ cup boiling water
1 tsp cornflour dissolved in
    1 Tbsp cold water

Mustard mash

2 Tbsp milk

6 medium potatoes, peeled and
    boiled until very soft
1 Tbsp fat-free cottage or
    cream cheese
2 Tbsp Dijon mustard
a generous pinch of salt and freshly
    ground black pepper

WHAT TO DO

1. Preheat the oven to 180 °C. Place the sausages in an ovenproof dish.
2. In a bowl, mix the mustard, honey, chutney, lemon juice and olive oil. Stir well and pour over the sausages, ensuring they are well coated.
3. Scatter over the thyme and bake for 25–30 minutes, rolling the sausages over once or twice during cooking.
4. Make the gravy using the juices from the cooked sausages. Tip the juices into a saucepan, add the gravy powder, water and cornflour paste, and simmer for about 5 minutes until thickened.
5. To make the mustard mash, combine all the ingredients and mash until light and fluffy.
6. Serve the sausages on a bed of mash and smothered in gravy.

SEAFOOD.

GRILLED SOY AND HONEY SALMON.

This is a Graham family favourite and few of the in-law tribe don't have it stashed away in their recipe files. I managed to get my 'outlaw' hands on a copy a while ago and have it very safely, and smugly, filed away. It is, after all, almost priceless, especially when lovingly cooked by Rob's chic and cheffy Aunty Sue on their little farm in Stellenbosch just outside Cape Town.

Serves 4 | **Preparation time** 5 minutes | **Cooking time** 10 minutes

WHAT YOU'LL NEED

2 sticks fresh lemongrass

¼ cup soy sauce

a handful of fresh coriander, stalks chopped and leaves set aside

2 cm piece fresh ginger, peeled and grated

4 cloves garlic, finely chopped

1 large or 2 medium salmon fillets, about 800 g in total

¼ cup runny honey

2 red chillies, deseeded and finely chopped

juice of 2 limes (about ¼ cup lime juice if you are using a bottle)

WHAT TO DO

1. 'Bruise' the lemongrass to release the flavour by bashing it with a bottle or in a pestle and mortar. Mix the lemongrass, soy sauce, coriander stalks, ginger and garlic in a large Ziploc bag or Tupperware, and add the salmon, making sure it is well coated in the mixture. Leave to marinate for 1 hour.
2. A few minutes before cooking, preheat the grill to its highest setting.
3. Remove the salmon from the marinade, drizzle with the honey and grill in an uncovered ovenproof dish for 10 minutes until golden.
4. Serve with the chopped chilli, coriander leaves and lime juice.

CORIANDER PESTO-BAKED HAKE
with tomato and dill salsa.

Serves 4 | **Preparation time** 15 minutes | **Cooking time** 12–15 minutes

WHAT YOU'LL NEED

4 medium hake fillets (or any white-fleshed fish you prefer)

4 tsp coriander pesto

4 tsp butter at room temperature

zest and juice of 1 lemon

a generous pinch of salt and freshly ground black pepper

2 lemons, cut into wedges

Tomato and dill salsa

2 ripe tomatoes, diced

1 clove garlic, finely chopped

2 Tbsp chopped fresh dill

½ red onion, peeled and finely chopped

1 avocado, peeled and roughly chopped

zest and juice of 1 lemon

1 Tbsp olive oil

a generous pinch of salt and freshly ground black pepper

WHAT TO DO

1. Preheat the oven to 200 °C.
2. Place each hake fillet on a square of tin foil large enough to generously wrap the fillet.
3. Mix the pesto, butter, lemon zest and juice, salt and pepper into a rough paste and use to baste each fillet on both sides.
4. Tightly wrap up the fillets and place in a shallow ovenproof dish. Bake for 12–15 minutes until the flesh flakes easily.
5. To make the salsa, mix all the ingredients in a small serving bowl.
6. Place each fish fillet parcel onto a warm plate for your guests to unwrap at the table. Serve with the lemon wedges and salsa on the side.

WELCOME TO SEARED TUNA HEAVEN.

Now if you bump into Noordhoek's most eligible bachelor walking down the street, there may be a few things you notice about him … his strapping good looks, his passion for rugby (and beer) (and wine) and his fast-talking, quick-thinking, sharp wit. You may not, however, easily conclude that up his sleeve he holds the key to every single woman's heart. And it's called Seared Tuna. Yip. Mr Michael Jenkins Esq. has foiled us all into giving him free meals for as long as we can remember and has only now revealed that he in fact has all the savoir-faire of a seasoned foodie. Now we could choose to be peeved that he has not chosen to reveal this hidden talent sooner, or we could just be eternally grateful that he finally chose to do so. I am going with the latter. And so will you. So, without further ado, I will leave the stage to the man of the moment …

Serves 4 | **Preparation time** 25 minutes | **Cooking time** 10 minutes

WHAT YOU'LL NEED

soy sauce
juice and zest of 1 lemon or lime
1 clove garlic, crushed
2 tsp grated fresh ginger
2 tsp brown sugar
2 Tbsp chopped fresh coriander
1 Tbsp olive oil
4 of the freshest tuna steaks you can find
salt and freshly ground black pepper to taste
¼ cup toasted sesame seeds
1 ripe avocado, peeled and roughly chopped

WHAT TO DO

1. Mix the soy sauce, lemon or lime juice and zest, garlic, ginger, sugar, coriander and olive oil in a bowl. Let this mixture stand for 20 minutes.
2. Heat a large frying pan over a medium heat and coat with non-stick cooking spray or 1 Tbsp olive oil. Test the pan with a small piece of tuna – you want it to sizzle immediately, but not burn.
3. Season one side of a tuna steak with salt and pepper and place seasoned-side down in the pan for 1 minute. Turn the steak and immediately spoon over a healthy dollop of the sauce. Give it 1 minute on the other side and transfer straight onto a heated plate. Repeat with the other steaks.
4. Garnish with the toasted sesame seeds and a couple of slices of avocado for the perfect finish. This is excellent served with a strawberry and spinach leaf salad (see page 62) and honey-roasted sweet potatoes (see page 143).

PRAWNS

in Thai green curry sauce.

You can't beat this for a speedy supper option. And I love the pretty plump pinkness of the prawns in the green curry.
Mom and I first made this together when she heroically came to Cape Town to help me test recipes for this book,
and it left us feeling very smug about life.

Serves 4 | **Preparation time** 5 minutes | **Cooking time** 15 minutes

WHAT YOU'LL NEED

1–2 Tbsp olive oil

1 onion, peeled and chopped

1 tsp chopped fresh ginger

1 Tbsp Thai green curry paste (or ½ Tbsp
for mild)

2 tsp brown sugar

2 cloves garlic, crushed

1 x 400 ml can coconut milk

a handful of fresh basil leaves,
roughly chopped

2 tsp fish sauce (not something you always
have in your pantry, but worth investing in and
it lasts really well)

juice of 1 lime

24 prawns, shelled (can be cooked directly
from frozen)

a handful of fresh coriander, roughly chopped

salt to taste

WHAT TO DO

1. Heat the oil in a frying pan or wok and cook the onion, ginger, curry paste, sugar and garlic until the onion is lightly golden. Add the coconut milk and simmer for 10 minutes.
2. Add the basil, fish sauce, lime juice and prawns, and cook for a further 3 minutes until the prawns are a rosy pink colour.
3. Spoon over fluffy basmati rice, garnish with the chopped coriander and season with salt.

SPICY GRUYÈRE-CRUSTED FISHCAKES
with watercress pesto.

These are seriously budget friendly and super-low maintenance, AND Rob gives them a 9/10 ... Gruyère is his absolute favourite cheese in the world, but you are welcome to use any other hard cheese, such as Parmesan. Grilled and with no flour, the only thing you need to forgive yourself for is a little grated cheese, now who can't manage that? However, for a really healthy option, you can leave off the cheese crust.

Serves 4 | **Preparation time** 5 minutes | **Cooking time** 25 minutes

WHAT YOU'LL NEED
450 g fish, such as hake

2 Tbsp milk

salt and freshly ground black pepper to taste

3 small sweet potatoes, peeled

2 Tbsp chopped fresh parsley

1 level tsp each of ground cumin, ground coriander and dried chilli flakes

juice and zest of 1 lemon

1 egg, lightly beaten

½ cup grated Gruyère cheese

olive oil for grilling

Watercress pesto
50 g fresh watercress, rinsed and thicker stalks removed

2 Tbsp pine nuts

3 Tbsp olive oil

juice of 1 lemon

1 clove garlic, chopped

WHAT TO DO
1. Preheat the oven to 190 °C.
2. Place the fish on the shiny side of a large sheet of tin foil, pour over the milk and sprinkle with a pinch of salt and pepper. Wrap up tightly and bake for 15 minutes.
3. Meanwhile, boil the sweet potatoes for 15 minutes until soft and easy to mash.
4. In a bowl, flake the fish, then mix in the mashed sweet potato, parsley, cumin, coriander, chilli, lemon juice, lemon zest and about half the beaten egg. Season with salt and pepper.
5. Shape the mixture into 12 patties and gently roll each in the cheese, coating top and bottom. Refrigerate for about 15 minutes or until you are ready to cook.
6. Heat the oven's grill. Place the fishcakes on an oven tray and drizzle with a little olive oil. Grill 5–7 minutes on each side, until golden and crispy.
7. To make the watercress pesto, blend all the ingredients for 2–3 minutes.
8. Serve the fishcakes with fresh asparagus and Caprese salad stacks (see page 66).

Note: These can be made the day before and left to chill in the fridge in an airtight container.

BEER-BASTED PRAWNS
with coriander cream sauce.

Serves 4 | **Preparation time** 5 minutes | **Cooking time** 6 minutes

WHAT YOU'LL NEED

24 prawns, with their shells on, legs and head removed and butterflied

½ cup beer (Mozambican if you can find it!)

2 Tbsp butter, melted (in the microwave for about 30 seconds)

2 cloves garlic, finely chopped

zest and juice of 1 lemon

1 tsp dried chilli flakes or 1 fresh chilli, deseeded and finely chopped

a handful each of fresh coriander and parsley, roughly chopped

Coriander cream sauce

¼ cup smooth cottage or cream cheese

1 Tbsp coriander pesto

WHAT TO DO

1. Preheat the oven's grill to its highest setting. Place the prawns in a shallow ovenproof dish and pour over the beer, melted butter, garlic, lemon zest, lemon juice and chilli.

2. Grill the prawns for 3 minutes on each side or until they take on a rosy pink colour.

3. To make the coriander cream sauce, mix the cheese and pesto in a small serving bowl.

4. Serve the prawns on heated plates and garnished with the chopped coriander and parsley and a dollop of coriander sauce on the side, accompanied by fluffy couscous stirred through with mint and lemon juice.

Note: To butterfly a prawn, cut a deep line along the belly, open it out and press down so that it's relatively flat. Alternatively, shell the prawns and cook on short skewers to serve as a snack.

MUSSELS

in tomato, chilli and basil sauce.

Serves 2 | Preparation time 5–10 minutes | Cooking time 10 minutes | Rob's rating 7.5/10

WHAT YOU'LL NEED

250 g black deshelled mussels
2 Tbsp olive oil
1–2 small red chillies, deseeded and finely chopped or ½ tsp dried chilli flakes
1 clove garlic, chopped
1 small onion, peeled and chopped
2 Tbsp lemon juice
1 x 410 g can chopped peeled tomatoes
a handful of roughly chopped fresh basil
2 ciabatta rolls
olive oil for drizzling
100 g Parmesan cheese, shaved
2 Tbsp chopped fresh parsley
salt and freshly ground black pepper to taste

WHAT TO DO

1. Rinse the mussels under warm water in a colander and set aside.
2. Heat the olive oil in a frying pan and fry the chilli, garlic and onion until golden.
3. Add the lemon juice and mussels to the pan, cover with a lid and cook for 1 minute.
4. Add the tomatoes and basil, and simmer for 5 minutes, stirring every now and then.
5. In the meantime, preheat the oven's grill to its highest setting, slice the ciabatta rolls in half and place under the grill for 2–3 minutes until golden. Drizzle with olive oil and top with Parmesan shavings.
6. Spoon the mussels in their sauce into warm bowls, garnish with the chopped parsley and season with a generous sprinkling of salt and pepper. Serve with the rolls on the side. Alternatively, serve over angel-hair pasta with a light rocket and baby spinach salad on the side.

Note: Although fresh is always better, this dish works well using frozen mussels rinsed under warm tap water.

PASTAS & RISOTTOS.

SMOKED SALMON LINGUINI.

*This. Is. Unbelievable. I got it through a recipe swap ages ago and, having given it a few new twists, I now want to put it on everything –
not just pasta, but little tarts and quiches and bruschetta, and anything else I can think up that would be a humble blank canvas for
this deliciousness.*

Serves 4 | Preparation time 5 minutes | Cooking time 10 minutes

WHAT YOU'LL NEED

⅔ x 500 g pkt linguini (or any long pasta of
your choice)
olive oil for drizzling
150 g smoked salmon, cut into strips
zest and juice of 1 lemon
2 Tbsp horseradish sauce
1 cup smooth cottage cheese
2 Tbsp mascarpone or crème fraîche
salt and freshly ground black pepper to taste
4 handfuls of watercress, roughly chopped

WHAT TO DO

1. Cook the pasta according to the packet instructions, drain, drizzle
   with olive oil and transfer to a large serving bowl.
2. Mix in the remaining ingredients, except the watercress.
3. Top each serving with a handful of chopped watercress.

why-he-married-me
BACON PASTA.

I know right, sad to think that Rob could be that shallow … Sometimes, though, I really do think that this was right up there with the other good attributes I may possess when he decided to pop the question. Well, whatever his reasoning, I can't find fault with his passion for this dish, except that he requests it so often that I can't believe we haven't killed it yet. I've been making it for so long that I honestly can't remember where I got the recipe from in the first place; I just recall stirring away over our two-plate stove at university and being delighted with the results …

Serves 4 | **Preparation time** 15 minutes | **Cooking time** 45 minutes | **Rob's rating** 10/10

WHAT YOU'LL NEED

250 g pasta (really thin spaghetti is our
household favourite)

3 Tbsp olive oil + more for drizzling

1 medium onion, peeled and chopped

½–1 tsp dried chilli flakes

1 tsp ground coriander

2 cloves garlic, chopped

1 x 250 g pkt bacon, chopped (I use kitchen
scissors, nice trick)

2 x 410 g cans chopped peeled tomatoes

2 Tbsp chutney or sweet chilli sauce

1 cup chopped courgettes (baby marrows)

1–2 tsp freshly ground black pepper

½ cup cream or plain yoghurt

2 Tbsp chopped fresh basil or parsley

WHAT TO DO

1. Cook the pasta according to the packet instructions, drain, drizzle with olive oil and set aside.

2. Heat the 3 Tbsp olive oil in a pot and brown the onion, chilli, coriander and garlic.

3. Add the bacon and brown that too before adding the tomatoes and chutney or sweet chilli sauce.

4. Bring to the boil, then reduce the heat and simmer for about 30 minutes until the sauce starts to thicken and changes to a rich brick-red colour.

5. Add the courgettes, pepper and cream or yoghurt, and simmer for a further 5 minutes.

6. Serve over the pasta and garnish with the fresh basil or parsley.

Note: You could easily add mushrooms to this dish or use chicken instead of bacon. You could also serve it with some crumbled feta sprinkled over the top.

CLASSIC CARBONARA
you have to try.

No one seems to know the exact origin of Spaghetti alla carbonara – spaghetti, coal-miner style. There are lots of anecdotal options: it was literally the favoured fare of coal miners; the black pepper bits resemble coal flakes; after WWII, Allied troops in the war-ravaged Italian countryside used powdered egg and bacon rations to season their pasta …

Whatever its origin, I have always thought carbonara is exquisite in its simplicity. Demure, humble, quietly going about its business of being one of the most iconic Italian dishes known to man. It really has no reason to brag, because its reputation precedes it. So much so that I bet many people don't try it at home, the risk of the eggs scrambling being enough to put anyone off, right? Well it shouldn't. There are just so many things right about this. For starters, I pinky promise that it takes as long to cook as the pasta takes to boil; it's far from fussy. And when you're done, you'll have a plate full of subtly flavoured, literally lip-smacking, creamy eggy-bacony deliciousness.

Serves 4 | **Preparation time** 5 minutes | **Cooking time** 10 minutes | **Rob's rating** 8.25/10
(Can you tell he takes his job very seriously? Getting technical!)

WHAT YOU'LL NEED

⅔ x 500 g pkt pasta (spaghetti or linguini is best)

2 Tbsp olive oil

1 x 250 g pkt bacon, chopped (I use kitchen scissors, much faster)

2 Tbsp white wine (optional)

2 eggs

¼ cup grated Parmesan cheese (I've also used Gruyère before)

2 Tbsp cream

½ tsp ground nutmeg

a pinch of salt and freshly ground black pepper

a handful of chopped fresh parsley

WHAT TO DO

1. Cook the pasta according to the packet instructions.
2. In the meantime, heat the olive oil in a frying pan and fry the bacon until lightly golden. Pour in the wine (if using) and cook for a further 2–3 minutes. Remove the pan from the heat and set aside.
3. In a jug, whisk the eggs, and then add the Parmesan and cream.
4. Once the pasta is cooked, drain it, reserving ¼ cup of the starchy cooking water. Tip the pasta into the pan with the bacon. Make sure the pan is not on either of the hot stove plates you have been using (you don't want the egg to scramble!).
5. Pour in the egg mixture and stir everything together until the pasta is well coated, adding in a little of the reserved pasta water to loosen things up if it's a little too sticky for your liking.
6. Sprinkle over the nutmeg, salt, pepper and parsley and serve with toasted crusty ciabatta topped with pesto and goat's cheese or just plain butter.

our favourite

LEBANESE LAMB PASTA.

So this really is an old favourite, and I have my dear friend Elizabeth to thank for it. We used to cook it during exams when we were at UCT together. It's budget friendly and super easy. Elizabeth is part Lebanese, so that's where that comes in. I suppose you could say that this is a loose adaptation of an old Lebanese family favourite (because no one cooks it quite like they do). You can use couscous instead of pasta if you prefer.

Serves 4 | **Preparation time** 15 minutes | **Cooking time** 45–50 minutes | **Rob's rating** 8/10

WHAT YOU'LL NEED

½ x 500 g pkt tagliatelle

3 Tbsp olive oil + extra for drizzling

2 cloves garlic, chopped

1 tsp dried chilli flakes or 1 fresh chilli, deseeded and chopped

750 g lamb, chopped

2 x 410 g cans chopped peeled tomatoes

2 Tbsp chutney or sweet chilli sauce

freshly ground black pepper and salt to taste

¼ cup chopped fresh parsley

WHAT TO DO

1. Cook the pasta according to the packet instructions, drain, drizzle with olive oil and set aside.

2. Heat the olive oil in a pot and brown the garlic, chilli and lamb. Add the tomatoes and chutney or sweet chilli sauce, and simmer for at least 45 minutes. The longer the better!

3. Season generously with freshly ground black pepper and add salt to taste.

4. Divide the pasta between warm bowls, ladle over the pasta sauce, sprinkle with parsley and serve with a simple side salad.

Note: I prefer to use lamb neck or chump chops, or both. Include the bones as they add more flavour.

MUSHROOM PASTA.

So. If you live in Cape Town and love food, chances are you've heard of The Food Barn Restaurant in Noordhoek. And if you haven't, well you must have been living under a rock or something, and I pity you. Anyway, their resident French chef is currently running cooking demonstrations, and I took my dear friend Debs there a couple of weeks ago. I can't even spell half the stuff that Chef Franck Dangereux (I have to ask him if that is for real) pulled together that day, but what I did take away with me was the exquisite cream sauce that he used for his fresh sage linguini. Oh, and how unpretentious he was, being a French chef and all. Fascinating. So, this is a very loose adaptation of Franck's sauce – any deliciousness is full credit to him and anything that's not you can lump me with.

Serves 4 | Preparation time 10 minutes | Cooking time 15 minutes

WHAT YOU'LL NEED

250 g pasta of your choice (I suggest penne)

olive oil for drizzling

¼ cup butter

1 clove garlic, chopped

2 rashers bacon, diced

4 cups chopped mushrooms (I use half brown and half button mushrooms)

½ cup cream or plain yoghurt

1–2 Tbsp balsamic vinegar

salt and freshly ground black pepper to taste

2 Tbsp chopped fresh parsley

WHAT TO DO

1. Cook the pasta according to the packet instructions, drain, drizzle with olive oil and set aside.
2. Heat the butter in a frying pan and brown the garlic and bacon.
3. Add the mushrooms (you can add an extra 1 Tbsp butter at this stage if there's not enough liquid for the mushrooms, as you don't want them to burn).
4. When the mushrooms start to turn a golden brown colour, add the cream or yoghurt followed by the balsamic vinegar and cook for a further 3–5 minutes, allowing the sauce to colour and thicken slightly. Season with salt and pepper to taste.
5. Serve the sauce over the pasta and garnish with the fresh parsley.

Note: Leave out the bacon for a vegetarian option.

SUMMERY LEMON AND ASPARAGUS RISOTTO.

I like to think of this as a brilliantly sharp and witty risotto. It's full of vibrant, zesty flavours, but possibly the best part about it is the ingenious trick of pre-boiling the risotto rice that I learnt from renowned Cape Town-based (and fellow Zimbabwean) chef Neill Anthony, which drastically cuts down the cooking (and stirring!) time.

Serves 4 | Preparation time 5 minutes | Cooking time 20 minutes

WHAT YOU'LL NEED

350 g risotto rice
2 Tbsp olive oil
1 Tbsp butter
1 onion, peeled and finely chopped
200 ml white wine
400 ml vegetable stock
about 24 asparagus spears, trimmed
juice of 1 lemon
¼ cup grated Parmesan cheese
100 g goat's cheese
salt and freshly ground black pepper to taste

WHAT TO DO

1. Bring about 2 cups water to the boil in a medium-sized pot. When the water is bubbling, add the risotto rice and cook for 5 minutes. Drain, do NOT rinse, and set aside.

2. Heat the oil and butter in another medium-sized pot over a medium-high heat and fry the onion for 3–4 minutes. Add the rice, stirring to coat in the oil and butter. Add the wine and stir for 2–3 minutes until absorbed.

3. Gradually add the stock, stirring and allowing each addition to absorb before adding the next.

4. Meanwhile, cook the asparagus spears in a pot of boiling water for about 4 minutes until just tender. Drain, refresh under cold water and set aside. The cold water will ensure that they stay nice and green.

5. After about 10 minutes, when the stock has been absorbed, add the asparagus, lemon juice, Parmesan and goat's cheese, and stir through gently. Season with salt and pepper, remove from the heat and cover for a few minutes before serving on warmed plates.

BAKED RISOTTO

with roasted butternut, goat's cheese and sage.

You hear that people? Baked, not stirred. Risotto is definitely one of the unsung heroes of the food world. And I'm pretty sure you'll agree with me if you give this a bash. One of the main reasons I think risotto is so fantastic is because I've discovered that it's your month-end best mate when the cupboard is bare or, as was our case today, when you've been away for a few days and have come home to an empty fridge. It is a very forgiving and accommodating friend to anything you can throw at it.

Serves 4 | **Preparation time** 10 minutes | **Cooking time** 45 minutes

WHAT YOU'LL NEED

1 cup peeled and cubed butternut
olive oil for drizzling
salt and freshly ground black pepper to taste
2 Tbsp olive oil
2 Tbsp butter
1 medium onion, peeled and finely chopped
1 clove garlic, chopped
1 Tbsp chopped fresh sage
1 cup Arborio (risotto) rice
½ cup white wine
700 ml chicken or vegetable stock
½ cup crumbled goat's cheese
⅓ cup grated Parmesan cheese (I have also used Gruyère before)
a dollop of mascarpone or crème fraîche

WHAT TO DO

1. Preheat the oven to 180 °C.
2. Place the butternut in an ovenproof dish, drizzle with olive oil and sprinkle with salt and pepper, and bake for 15–20 minutes until soft. When the butternut is done, purée half of it.
3. Heat the olive oil and butter in an ovenproof pot and fry the onion and garlic for about 5 minutes until translucent. Add half the sage and all the risotto, stirring until well coated. Then pour in the wine and simmer for 5 minutes.
4. Stir well and add the stock. Cover and cook in the oven for 15–20 minutes until the rice is soft.
5. Add the butternut purée to the risotto along with the goat's cheese, most of the Parmesan, the remaining cubed butternut and the remaining sage, and stir through.
6. Serve with the remaining Parmesan sprinkled on top, as well as a dollop of mascarpone or crème fraîche.

SIDES.

Honey-roasted sweet potatoes.

honey-roasted
SWEET POTATOES.

Serves 4 | **Preparation time** 5 minutes | **Cooking time** 35–40 minutes

WHAT YOU'LL NEED

4 medium sweet potatoes, peeled and roughly chopped into wedges

1 Tbsp honey

WHAT TO DO

1. Preheat the oven to 180 °C. Evenly distribute the raw potato wedges in a roasting dish and drizzle over the honey.
2. Roast on the middle shelf of the oven for 35–40 minutes until soft and golden. If you like, you can make them extra crispy and golden by turning on the grill for the last 3–4 minutes.

Note: Make sweet potato fries by peeling and slicing the potatoes into thin French-fry slivers and spreading them thinly in a large, shallow ovenproof dish. Bake as they are or with a drizzle of olive oil until golden and slightly crispy.

SWEETCORN MASHED POTATO.

Serves 4 | **Preparation time** 10 minutes | **Cooking time** 15 minutes

WHAT YOU'LL NEED

4 large potatoes, peeled and roughly chopped

⅔ cup milk

2 Tbsp butter

½ tsp ground nutmeg

180 g whole kernel corn, drained

a generous pinch of salt and freshly ground black pepper

WHAT TO DO

1. Boil the potatoes in a medium-sized pot for about 15 minutes until very soft. Drain and return to the warm pot.
2. Add the milk, butter and nutmeg, and mash until fluffy. Mix in the corn, salt and pepper.

Note: Make garlic and dill mash by leaving out the nutmeg and corn, and adding 1–2 chopped cloves garlic and 2–3 Tbsp chopped fresh dill.

Sides. **143**

PEANUT BUTTER BUTTERNUT FROM THE BUSH.

Hello lovelies! I shan't bang on any more about our recent trip to the Kenyan bush, I think I have done quite enough of that for the time being. (I hear your collective sigh of relief.) I shall, however, share with you our latest BBQ bonanza in the form of fire-roasted butternut smothered in peanut butter. Sounds random I know, but it's honest-to-goodnessly delicious – even back home in your yuppie kitchen sans campfire, stars and bush.

P.S. It must be fate that this has arrived the day before National Braai Day here in South Africa. Lekker boet.

P.P.S. You're welcome.

Serves 4 | **Preparation time** 3 minutes | **Cooking time** 45 minutes

WHAT YOU'LL NEED

1 large butternut, halved and deseeded

3–4 Tbsp peanut butter

WHAT TO DO

1. Prepare some good camping-fire coals or preheat the oven to 180 °C.
2. Make a few criss-crosses with a knife over the surface of the butternut halves and spread liberally with the peanut butter.
3. Wrap the butternut halves each in their own tin foil with the shiny side facing inwards.
4. Place on the coals or in the oven and leave for 45 minutes until soft. Unwrap and serve.

POLENTA

with roasted butternut and crispy sage.

Serves 4–6 | **Preparation time** 5 minutes | **Cooking time** 25 minutes + 15 minutes

WHAT YOU'LL NEED

750 g butternut, peeled and diced

3 Tbsp olive oil

1 cup polenta

a pinch of salt and freshly ground black pepper

2 Tbsp butter

2 Tbsp chopped fresh sage leaves

⅓–½ cup grated Parmesan cheese

WHAT TO DO

1. Preheat the oven to 190 °C and line a shallow ovenproof dish with baking paper.
2. Spread out the butternut on the baking paper and drizzle with 2 Tbsp of the olive oil, stirring to coat well. Bake for 25 minutes until tender, turning halfway through.
3. Cook the polenta according to the packet instructions, adding the salt and pepper. It should take 12–15 minutes to achieve a medium consistency or slightly longer for a thicker consistency.
4. Roughly mash the roasted butternut with a fork, add it to the polenta and stir until heated through.
5. In a small saucepan, melt the butter over a medium heat and simmer until it browns slightly. Add the sage and fry until crispy.
6. Sprinkle the sage and Parmesan over the polenta and serve immediately.

have your way with

COUSCOUS.

Rob loves couscous. Thankfully. Because you can honestly have a steaming bowl on the table in less than 5 minutes, it looks great, keeps well in the fridge for lunch the next day and is leftovers' best friend, because you can chuck almost anything into the mix and the couscous is ever-obliging and welcoming.

Serves 4 | **Preparation time** 2 minutes | **Cooking time** 3 minutes. I kid you not.

WHAT YOU'LL NEED

1½ cups couscous
2 cups boiling chicken or vegetable stock
a knob of butter (optional)
a handful of all or some of the following:
pumpkin seeds, chickpeas, crumbled feta,
chopped sun-dried or cherry tomatoes,
chopped avocado
handfuls of some or all of these roughly
chopped fresh herbs: rocket, coriander,
mint, parsley
a small handful of roughly chopped or
flaked almonds
2 Tbsp lemon juice or red wine vinegar
salt and freshly ground black pepper to taste

WHAT TO DO

1. Pour the uncooked couscous into a large bowl and cover with the stock. Cover and allow to stand for 3 minutes.
2. Test a small mouthful; it should be quite light and fluffy. Stir loosely with a fork (you don't want to turn it into mush) and, if you like, add a knob of butter at this stage.
3. Add the remaining ingredients, stir through gently and serve.

Note: A favourite variation is to mix 2 Tbsp basil or coriander pesto into the plain couscous and serve with almost any meat.

CHILLI AND LIME-ROASTED CORN.

Serves 4 | **Preparation time** 5 minutes | **Cooking time** 25 minutes

WHAT YOU'LL NEED

4 ears fresh corn
¼ cup butter
1 tsp dried chilli flakes
zest and juice of 1 lime

WHAT TO DO

1. Preheat the oven to 180 °C. (If you are using a braai or barbecue, you'll want low coals.)
2. Wrap each ear of corn in tin foil and roast in the oven or over the coals for 25 minutes.
3. While the corn is roasting, mix the butter with the chilli and lime zest.
4. Unwrap the ears of corn, rub with the soft butter mixture, and squeeze over some lime juice.

MINTED PEA PURÉE.

Serves 4 | **Preparation time** 5 minutes | **Cooking time** 5 minutes

WHAT YOU'LL NEED

2 cups water
1 cup frozen peas
¼ cup plain yoghurt
¼ cup vegetable stock
1 clove garlic, crushed
2 Tbsp mint leaves
salt and freshly ground black pepper to taste

WHAT TO DO

1. Bring the water to the boil, add the peas and cook for 3–4 minutes until just soft.
2. Drain and add the yoghurt, stock, garlic and mint. Blend with a stick blender or in a food processor until smooth.
3. Season with salt and pepper, and serve.

Chilli and lime-roasted corn.

Mashed chickpeas and roasted butternut.

MASHED CHICKPEAS AND ROASTED BUTTERNUT
with garlic, chilli and cumin.

Serves 4 | **Preparation time** 10 minutes | **Cooking time** 15 minutes

WHAT YOU'LL NEED
1 cup peeled and cubed butternut
1 Tbsp olive oil
1 tsp ground cumin
1 x 410 g can chickpeas, drained
1 clove garlic, finely chopped
½–1 tsp dried chilli flakes
1 Tbsp chopped fresh coriander or parsley

WHAT TO DO
1. In a microwave-proof dish with a lid, microwave the butternut on High for 5–6 minutes until soft.
2. Preheat the oven to 200 °C. Transfer the butternut to a medium-sized ovenproof dish, drizzle with the olive oil and cumin, toss so that it is evenly coated and bake for 10–15 minutes until golden. Add the chickpeas for the last 2–3 minutes to warm through.
3. In a warmed serving bowl, roughly mash the butternut and chickpeas together with the garlic and chilli. Garnish with coriander or parsley.

ROAST BUTTERNUT
with caramelised onion relish.

Serves 4 | **Preparation time** 10 minutes | **Cooking time** 20–25 minutes

WHAT YOU'LL NEED
3 cups peeled and cubed butternut
1 Tbsp butter
1 red onion, peeled and roughly chopped
1 Tbsp olive oil
1 Tbsp balsamic vinegar
1 Tbsp honey
salt and freshly ground black pepper to taste

WHAT TO DO
1. In a microwave-proof dish with a lid, microwave the butternut on High for 5–6 minutes until it can be easily pierced with a fork.
2. Preheat the oven to 200 °C. Heat the butter in a small saucepan over a medium-high heat and fry the onion for 10 minutes until golden.
3. Transfer the butternut to a medium-sized ovenproof dish, drizzle with the olive oil and bake for 10–15 minutes until golden.
4. Remove from the oven, toss in the caramelised onion, balsamic vinegar and honey, and season with salt and pepper to taste.

Sides. 151

DESSERTS.

MALVA PUDDING.

Now THIS is the stuff memories are made of. I grew up on Mom's homemade malva pudding, fresh out the oven after a roast Sunday lunch. If you're not in the know, malva pudding is a ubiquitous South African dessert originally of Dutch origin, and it's comfort food personified, as good as a hug from Mom herself. (Well, almost!) I have added my own touch to this one by including very special South African Amarula liqueur (a creamy liqueur similar to Baileys), which gives it a sneaky little kick.

Serves 8 | **Preparation time** 15 minutes | **Baking time** 45–60 minutes

WHAT YOU'LL NEED

1 cup cake flour
1 tsp bicarbonate of soda
a generous pinch of salt
1 egg
1 cup sugar
1 Tbsp apricot jam
1 Tbsp melted butter
1 tsp vinegar or lemon juice
1 cup milk

Sauce

50 ml cream
100 ml Amarula liqueur or regular cream
½ cup milk
1 cup sugar
½ cup hot water
½ cup butter

WHAT TO DO

1. Preheat the oven to 180 °C and line a baking dish with baking paper.
2. Sift the flour, bicarbonate of soda and salt into a bowl.
3. In a separate bowl, cream the egg and sugar, and then add the apricot jam, butter and vinegar or lemon juice.
4. Add the milk and flour to the egg mixture and beat well.
5. Pour into the baking dish, cover with tin foil and bake for 45–60 minutes until lightly golden.
6. To make the sauce, melt all the ingredients together and pour over the pudding as soon as it comes out of the oven.
7. Serve with whipped or double cream or vanilla custard.

Note: You can make this in advance and freeze, thawing and reheating before serving. You can also freeze leftovers for use at a later stage.

mini molten
CHOCOLATE CAKES.

Serves 8 | **Preparation time** 10 minutes | **Baking time** 10–12 minutes

WHAT YOU'LL NEED

300 g dark chocolate, roughly chopped
50 g unsalted butter, softened
150 g icing sugar
4 eggs
1 tsp vanilla extract
2 Tbsp cake flour
50 g white chocolate, roughly chopped

WHAT TO DO

1. Preheat the oven to 200 °C and lightly grease eight holes in a muffin or cupcake tin with a little butter.
2. Melt the dark chocolate in a saucepan over a low heat, stirring regularly so that you get a silky texture. Allow to cool slightly.
3. Cream together the butter and icing sugar in a mixing bowl and slowly add the eggs and vanilla extract.
4. Add the flour, mix gently and then add the melted chocolate. Mix a little more until it's nice and smooth, and then stir in the white chocolate bits.
5. Divide the mixture between the holes in the tin and bake for 10–12 minutes. Remove the cakes from the tin as soon as possible and serve with whipped cream.

Notes: You can make the mixture, pour it into the tin and keep refrigerated for a good couple of hours before baking, a great time-saving option if you are having people round. If you do this, just bake for an extra 2 minutes.

These little puddings freeze beautifully. Thaw for 1 hour before serving and reheat in the microwave.

CRISPY GINGER, PEAR AND APPLE TART.

Serves 6–8 | **Preparation time** 15 minutes | **Baking time** 20–25 minutes

WHAT YOU'LL NEED

6 sheets phyllo pastry

¼ cup melted butter

4–5 Tbsp ground or crushed almonds

seeds of 1 vanilla pod or 1 tsp vanilla essence or extract

2 Tbsp castor sugar

1 Tbsp grated fresh ginger

6 just-ripe, slightly firm pears, peeled, cored and thinly sliced

2 apples, peeled, cored and thinly sliced

1 Tbsp muscovado or brown sugar

2 Tbsp slivered almonds

WHAT TO DO

1. Preheat the oven to 180 °C and grease a 25 x 15 cm baking dish.

2. Layer the phyllo pastry sheets in the dish, brushing each layer with melted butter. Trim the edges with kitchen scissors so that they are just level with the height of the dish.

3. Toss the ground almonds, vanilla, castor sugar, ginger, pears and apples in a large mixing bowl to coat evenly.

4. Scatter evenly over the pastry case, and sprinkle with the muscovado or brown sugar and slivered almonds.

5. Bake in the middle of the oven for 20–25 minutes until the pastry is golden and crispy. Turn up the temperature to 200 °C for the last few minutes to crisp the tart.

6. Serve at room temperature with whipped cream. I like to add a dash of Amarula liqueur to my cream before whipping.

Note: You can use peaches and nectarines instead of pears and apples.

MINI PAVLOVAS

with white chocolate mousse and berry coulis.

Makes 30–40 meringues I **Preparation time** 15 minutes I **Baking time** 45–50 minutes

WHAT YOU'LL NEED

1 egg white

250 g castor sugar

2 tsp vinegar (regular white wine vinegar or apple cider vinegar)

2 Tbsp boiling water

1 tsp vanilla essence

2 tsp baking powder

White chocolate mousse and berry coulis filling

100 g white chocolate

1 Tbsp milk

150 ml double cream

1 cup frozen mixed berries, defrosted

fresh berries for serving

Note: For a large pavlova, make a circular base of meringue mixture 15–20 cm in diameter, smooth out gently with a spoon and then dollop larger meringues around the edge to make a 'wall'.

WHAT TO DO

1. Preheat the oven to 120 °C and line two baking trays with baking paper.
2. Beat the egg white with an electric mixer for 2–3 minutes until peaks form, and then gradually add the sugar, beating all the while. While still beating, add the remaining ingredients one at a time, except the baking powder.
3. Beat well for a further 10 minutes until stiff and glossy white, then gently fold in the baking powder with a fork.
4. Spoon teaspoon-sized dollops of the meringue mixture onto the lined baking trays, each about 2 cm apart.
5. Using the back of a teaspoon, make a small 'crater' in the middle of each meringue, which will be for the filling at a later stage. Have a cup of hot water handy to dip the spoon into between each one so that you have a clean spoon for each meringue.
6. Bake for 45–50 minutes and then switch off the oven, but leave the meringues in until cold.
7. To make the mousse, slowly melt the chocolate with the milk in a small saucepan, whisk until smooth, then leave to cool. Whip the cream and fold into the chocolate mixture. Refrigerate until ready to serve.
8. Blend the defrosted berries in a food processor.
9. Just before serving, fill each pavlova case with about 1 heaped tsp mousse, drizzle over about 1 Tbsp berry coulis and garnish with a few fresh berries. It's important to only fill the pavlova cases just before eating, otherwise they risk going soggy.

WHOLE LEMON TART.

You can make this tart the day before and reheat slightly in the oven before serving.

Serves 6 | **Preparation time** 20–30 minutes | **Baking time** 30 minutes

WHAT YOU'LL NEED

Sweet shortcrust pastry

1½ cups all-purpose or cake flour

½ cup icing sugar

a pinch of salt

125 g cold butter

1 egg

⅔ tsp vanilla extract or 1 tsp vanilla essence

1 Tbsp milk

Filling

1 lemon, chopped small, rind included but seeds removed

1½ cups sugar

1 egg

1 egg yolk

1½ Tbsp cornflour

125 g butter, melted and at room temperature

WHAT TO DO

1. To make the pastry, sift the flour, icing sugar and salt in a large mixing bowl to remove any lumps.
2. Work the butter into the flour with your hands, breaking it up, then whisk by hand until the mixture resembles breadcrumbs.
3. Add the egg, vanilla and milk, and mix gently. Try to avoid over-working the dough. Form into a ball, wrap in clingfilm and refrigerate for about 15 minutes.
4. To make the filling, blend the chopped lemon in a blender and add the sugar in about four stages, mixing in between each addition.
5. Tip into a mixing bowl and add the egg, egg yolk, cornflour and melted butter. Mix well.
6. Preheat the oven to 160 °C. Lightly grease a tart tin or glass ovenproof dish (about 15 x 10 cm).
7. Roll out the pastry on a lightly floured surface to about 5 mm thick and use to line the tin or dish. Place in the freezer for 20 minutes (to avoid blind-baking).
8. Remove from the freezer, pour in the filling and bake for 15 minutes. Turn up the heat to 180 °C and bake for a further 15 minutes.
9. Allow to cool to room temperature when it will be perfectly ready to serve with fresh cream.

Notes: Instead of making the pastry from scratch, you can use a 400 g roll of readymade shortcrust pastry, thawed and rolled out slightly thinner. You can double the pastry and freeze half for up to two months to use when you need it. For easy filling and baking, freeze the dough already in a pie dish.

white chocolate and raspberry
MILLE-FEUILLE.

Mille-feuille is French for 'thousand layers' and this traditional French dessert is more than just a pretty face. It's also really versatile, and you can make it work with dark chocolate and almost any combination of fruits. Banana is another favourite of mine.

Serves 4 I **Preparation time** 10 minutes I **Baking time** 15 minutes

WHAT YOU'LL NEED

1 x 400 g roll readymade puff pastry, thawed
¼ cup melted butter
1 cup cream
1 cup fresh raspberries (or strawberries)
300 g white chocolate, roughly broken into chunks
1 Tbsp milk
a sprinkling of toasted almonds
4 large mint leaves
1 Tbsp icing sugar

WHAT TO DO

1. Preheat the oven to 180 °C. Line a baking tray with baking paper.
2. Roll out the pastry on a floured surface and brush with the melted butter. Cut into eight even rectangles. Place on the lined tray, about 5 mm apart, and bake for 10–12 minutes until lightly golden.
3. Meanwhile, whip the cream until light and fluffy, and refrigerate.
4. Crush half the berries in a blender to make a berry coulis and set aside.
5. Microwave the chocolate and milk for 1 minute and then whisk until the chocolate is completely melted, smooth and glossy.
6. Remove the pastry from the oven and allow to cool before lifting each square gently from the baking paper using a sharp utensil.
7. Assemble each dessert as follows on individual plates: a layer of pastry, a layer of whipped cream and a drizzle of berry coulis. Repeat the layers. Drizzle melted white chocolate over the top, scatter over fresh berries and toasted almonds, and add a mint leaf. Sift icing sugar over and serve. You may leave off the chocolate and simply decorate with fresh berries as shown.

GRANADILLA CHEESECAKE

in a glass.

Serves 4 | Preparation time 5–10 minutes

WHAT YOU'LL NEED

1 Tbsp butter

⅓ cup well-crushed biscuits, preferably ginger

about 1 heaped cup fat-free cream cheese at room temperature

½ cup crème fraîche

1 Tbsp icing sugar

1 Tbsp lemon juice

zest of ½ lemon

1 tsp vanilla essence

1 small can granadilla pulp (about ⅓ cup)

1 Tbsp chopped fresh mint leaves (optional)

2 Tbsp toasted slivered almonds (or any nuts of your choice) (optional)

WHAT TO DO

1. Melt the butter in the microwave for 15–20 seconds, add to the crushed biscuits in a mixing bowl and mix well. Divide the mixture between four pretty glasses or small dessert dishes.
2. Beat the cream cheese and crème fraîche together until light and fluffy, and then fold in the icing sugar, lemon juice, lemon zest and vanilla essence.
3. Spoon the cream mixture into each glass on top of the biscuit layer and top with granadilla pulp. Refrigerate until serving garnished with the chopped mint and toasted almonds.

Note: The easiest way to crush the biscuits is to put them in a Ziploc bag and bash with a rolling pin or wine bottle.

PEARS POACHED IN RED WINE

with vanilla mascarpone.

Serves 6 | **Preparation time** 10 minutes | **Cooking time** 25 minutes

WHAT YOU'LL NEED

½ bottle red wine

1 cup castor sugar

1 cinnamon stick, halved or

½ tsp ground cinnamon

1 tsp vanilla essence

6 whole just-ripe pears, peeled but with
stalk intact

6 sprigs of fresh mint

Vanilla mascarpone

½ cup mascarpone

½ tsp vanilla essence

1 Tbsp icing sugar

WHAT TO DO

1. In a large saucepan over a medium-high heat, simmer the wine, castor sugar, cinnamon and vanilla essence, stirring occasionally, for about 10 minutes.

2. Meanwhile, place the peeled pears in a covered dish and microwave on High for 5 minutes. Add the pears, along with the juices that will have collected in the microwave dish, to the saucepan and simmer for a further 5 minutes, turning now and then.

3. Remove the pears with a slotted spoon and set aside. Continue boiling the liquid for another 5 minutes to further reduce until syrupy. Remove from the heat and allow to cool slightly. Don't forget to remove the cinnamon stick if used.

4. To make the vanilla mascarpone, whisk all the ingredients together.

5. Serve each pear drenched in the cooled syrup, topped with a dollop of vanilla mascarpone and garnished with a sprig of fresh mint.

Note: These can be made a day or two in advance and refrigerated. Just reheat the pears in the microwave.

GINGER, CRANBERRY AND ALMOND SEMIFREDDO.

Semifreddo in Italian literally means 'half cold' and it's kind of half ice cream too. There are a few noteworthy things about this little dessert that will have you swooning … I've left out the faff of beating eggs, and I've used single cream instead of double, and fat-free yoghurt instead of Greek to shave off a few calories. Oh, and did I mention that it takes about 7 minutes to make?

Serves 6 | **Preparation time** 7 minutes | **Freezing time** 4 hours

WHAT YOU'LL NEED

3 Tbsp runny honey

1 tsp vanilla essence

300 ml fat-free plain yoghurt

¼ cup finely chopped almonds, lightly toasted in a dry pan

2 Tbsp finely chopped preserved ginger

1 cup cream

⅔ cup dried cranberries

2 Tbsp preserved ginger syrup

WHAT TO DO

1. Line a small loaf tin with clingfilm, so that there is enough to fold over and cover the mixture when you pour it in.
2. Mix the honey and vanilla essence into the yoghurt and set aside.
3. In a food processor, pulse the almonds and ginger (separately) if they are not already quite finely chopped.
4. Whisk the cream until it starts to form stiff peaks, then gently fold in all the ingredients and pour into the loaf tin.
5. Freeze for a minimum of 4 hours, removing 20–30 minutes before serving.
6. As a serving suggestion, slice into 2 cm-thick slices and serve with a sprig of mint or fresh berries on the side.

Note: The variations are endless – swap the cranberries, ginger and almonds for crushed mixed berries, or even peanut butter and melted chocolate! Just follow the basic quantity guidelines above.

AFTER DINNER BITES.

For when a full-on dessert is just too much …

HONEY-SPICED FIGS
with orange wafers.

Serves 4–6 | **Preparation time** 10 minutes | **Baking time** 10 minutes

WHAT YOU'LL NEED

6 small fresh figs
6 tsp mascarpone
150 g sugar
125 g golden syrup
100 g soft butter
juice of 1 orange
125 g cake flour, sifted
1 Tbsp honey
½ cinnamon stick

WHAT TO DO

1. Gently cut across the crown of each fig, cutting two-thirds of the way down. Squeeze the base and the top should open like a flower. Stuff each with 1 tsp of mascarpone and refrigerate.
2. Preheat the oven to 170 °C and line a baking tray with baking paper.
3. In a small saucepan, melt together the sugar, syrup, butter and orange juice. Remove from the heat and stir in the flour. Spoon the mixture onto the baking paper and spread out evenly. Bake for about 10 minutes until golden. Allow to cool before cutting or breaking into wafers.
4. Just before serving, heat the honey with the cinnamon stick in a small microwavable jug for about 25 seconds. Remove the cinnamon and drizzle the spiced honey over the figs. Serve with the orange wafers on the side.

WHITE CHOCOLATE AND GINGER BISCUIT TILES.

Makes 12 | **Preparation time** 10 minutes | **Cooling time** 2 hours

WHAT YOU'LL NEED

200 g white chocolate

⅓ cup crushed ginger biscuits

WHAT TO DO

1. Line a baking tray with baking paper.
2. Melt the chocolate in the microwave for 30 seconds. Stir well until the chocolate melts, microwaving for an extra 15 seconds if necessary. It should be smooth and silky.
3. Stir in the crushed biscuits and pour the mixture onto the baking paper, spreading it out as thinly as possible in a rough square.
4. Refrigerate for about 2 hours, before slicing into tiles to serve on a small platter.

MASCARPONE-STUFFED DATES.

Serves 4 | **Preparation time** 10 minutes

WHAT YOU'LL NEED

12–16 fresh dates

12–16 whole almonds (optional)

½ cup mascarpone

1 Tbsp icing sugar

1 tsp vanilla essence

1–2 Tbsp unsweetened cocoa powder

WHAT TO DO

1. Make a lengthways slit in each date and remove the stones, without cutting the dates completely in half.
2. Toast the almonds, if using, in a small frying pan over a medium heat, being careful not to burn them.
3. In a bowl, whisk the mascarpone, icing sugar and vanilla essence.
4. Spoon the mascarpone into the dates, close them loosely and top with an almond. Arrange on a plate and sift over the cocoa powder.

Note: The stuffed dates can be refrigerated overnight and then just brought to room temperature before dusting with cocoa.

White chocolate and ginger biscuit tiles.

DINKY CHOCOLATE TRUFFLES.

Makes 25 | **Preparation time** 10 minutes | **Cooling time** 30 minutes

WHAT YOU'LL NEED

150 ml cream

100 g good-quality dark chocolate, chopped

1 Tbsp butter

2 Tbsp cocoa powder

2 Tbsp grated white chocolate

2 Tbsp crushed mixed nuts (I like pistachios and almonds)

WHAT TO DO

1. Heat the cream in a saucepan until just below boiling point. Remove from the heat and add the chocolate and butter. Stir until the chocolate melts and you have a silky consistency.
2. Pour the mixture into a dish and refrigerate for about 30 minutes, until the chocolate is just slightly soft and workable.
3. Place the cocoa powder, white chocolate and nuts onto three separate plates. Have a cup of hot water and two teaspoons at the ready.
4. Scoop out a large teaspoon of chocolate and, using the other spoon or your hands, roll into a little ball, then roll in a topping of your choice to coat evenly. Repeat until you have a variety of coated truffles, place on a platter and return to the fridge until serving.

Notes: Divide the chocolate mixture in half, leaving one half plain and adding 2 Tbsp peanut butter or half a finely chopped, deseeded fresh chilli to the other.

The chocolate mixture can also be made up to a week in advance and kept in the fridge. Leave at room temperature for about 30 minutes before working with it.

MEALS FOR A MONTH.

To make your life simpler, I've put together this handy guide that includes speedy suppers, easy week-night dessert options, delicious lazy weekend meals and a selection of wines to enjoy with them. Enjoy!

The wine pairings were magnanimously provided by my friends at Under The Influence in Cape Town. Under The Influence is a wine community that loves great wine and learning more about it. Through Under The Influence, you can buy incredible wines from selected producers, meet the new First Growths, join fun and interactive wine tastings and mini courses, and watch their riveting online wine videos, especially tailored for you by the Wine Bandits! For more information, visit http://undertheinfluence.co.za

SPEEDY SUPPERS

Mondays

Eating meat-free on Mondays is now a global phenomenon and something I'm proud to support. The UN's top climate scientist, Rajendra Pachauri, states that 'People should consider eating less meat as a way of combating global warming. UN figures suggest that meat production puts more greenhouse gases into the atmosphere than transport.'

1. **Roasted butternut and sweetcorn quesadillas (p 44) served with a crunchy side salad**
Enjoy with a lightly wooded Chardonnay, such as the Jordan Barrel Fermented Chardonnay.

2. **Why-he-married-me bacon pasta (p 132)**
A superb option with a wooded Chardonnay, such as the Paul Cluver Chardonnay.

3. **Carrot and coriander soup (p 72) served with cheesy croutons** (sprinkle crusty bread with Parmesan and place under the grill for 3–4 minutes)
The beautiful aromatic flavours in this dish will pair incredibly well with a Viognier. Give the Lismore Viognier a bash!

4. **Cheese and tomato tart with basil cream sauce (p 40) served with a crunchy side salad**
This dish has an opulent mouth feel and needs a white wine to match, so try the Rudera Robusto Chenin Blanc.

Tuesdays

1. **Baby potato salad (p 65) served with a readymade roast chicken**
A wonderful pairing with a roast chicken dish is a Pinot Noir. Give the Paradyskloof Pinot Noir a whirl.

2. **Seared tuna (p 122) served with strawberry and spinach leaf salad (p 62)**
The addition of strawberries means there is only one pairing here and that is a light Pinot Noir packed with red fruit. Try the new Sutherland Pinot Noir from Thelema.

3. **Classic carbonara (p 135)**
Combine the smoky flavours in this dish with a smoky wine, perhaps a delicious Syrah like the Stark-Condé.

4. **Lemon and rosemary grilled lamb chops with pea and mint purée (p 103) served with honey-roasted sweet potatoes (p 143)**

The mint and herbaceous flavours in this dish will pair beautifully with a Cabernet Sauvignon. Try the boutique estate Belfield's Magnifica Cabernet Sauvignon.

Wednesdays

1. **Pea, courgette and mint soup (p 75) served with fresh crusty bread and goat's cheese**

This is not easy to pair, but can be braved with a full-bodied Chardonnay, such as the De Wetshof Bateleur Chardonnay.

2. **Prawns in Thai green curry sauce (p 123) served with fluffy basmati rice**

This is also not the easiest pairing, but a milder curry can be paired with the Paul Cluver Gewürztraminer, which is packed with rich fruit flavours.

3. **Creamy Dijon chicken (p 79) served with mashed regular or sweet potato and green peas**

When in doubt, when it comes to South African white wines, go for a Chenin Blanc, and with this dish the wooded yet elegant De Morgenzon Chenin Blanc would be a sure bet.

4. **Coriander pesto-baked hake with tomato and dill salsa (p 120) served with boiled baby potatoes**

A superb Chardonnay contestant this one, so try out a wooded one like the Oak Valley Chardonnay.

Thursdays

1. **15-minute lemon chicken skewers (p 84)**

For a quick meal, enjoy a quick and racy Sauvignon Blanc, such as the Steenberg H.M.S. Rattlesnake.

2. **Crustless bacon and spinach tart (p 112) served with a crunchy side salad**

Try a delectable Pinot Noir or a lighter Merlot here, perhaps the Newton Johnson Pinot Noir.

3. **Smoked salmon linguini (p 131)**

This is lovely, full-flavoured Sauvignon Blanc territory. Try the delicious Iona Sauvignon Blanc.

4. **Sticky pork bangers with creamy mustard mash (p 116)**

Bring out the spicy and full-flavoured Shiraz! Try the engaging Lammershoek Syrah.

Fridays

1. **Summery lemon and asparagus risotto (p 139)**

Asparagus is a wine's enemy, unless you are a Sauvignon Blanc! Give it a bash with a Durbanville Hills or Graham Beck Pheasants' Run Sauvignon Blanc, both packed with asparagus.

2. **Mussels in tomato, chilli and basil sauce (p 129) served with chunks of toasted ciabatta**

This is truly food fit for a king, so crack open some pink bubbly, perhaps a Ross Gower Brut Rosé.

3. **Greek lamb and feta burgers (p 93) served with honey-roasted sweet potatoes (p 143)**

Posh beef burgers deserve a posh Bordeaux-style red blend. Give the De Toren Z a whirl; it's the best posh-burger wine in town!

4. **Lamb pitas with lemony salsa (p 100)**

Cabernet Sauvignon and lamb are just the perfect pairing. Try out the Waterford Cabernet Sauvignon with this beautiful dish.

SPEEDY WEEK-NIGHT SWEET TREATS

1. **Mini molten chocolate cakes (p 154)**
2. **Granadilla cheesecake in a glass (p 162)**
3. **Pears poached in red wine (p 165)**
4. **Raspberry and white chocolate mille-feuille (p 161)**
5. **Honey-spiced figs with orange wafers (p 167)**
6. **White chocolate and ginger biscuit tiles (p 168)**
7. **Dinky chocolate truffles (p 171)**
8. **Mascarpone-stuffed dates (p 168)**

Desserts are not often accompanied by wine, but do yourself a favour and try pairing certain dessert wines. Avoid just plain 'Late Harvests', as these can be like drinking pure concentrate juice! You want a 'Noble Late Harvest', which indicates the grapes have gone through a very selective process to create intense, yet fresh, honeyed flavours. Just sublime stuff. For a special treat, give the Paul Cluver Noble Late Harvest a try, along with the Vin de Constance.

LAZY WEEKEND FOOD

1. **Roast chicken (p 80) with sweetcorn mashed potato (p 143), followed by malva pudding (p 153)**
   Go for a complex white blend from the Swartland for this one. Give the Lammershoek Roulette Blanc a try!
2. **Mustard and garlic roast fillet (p 105) with honey-roasted sweet potatoes (p 143) and warm beetroot salad (p 61), followed by whole lemon tart (p 158)**
   These intense flavours demand an intense wine partner. Shiraz foots the bill! Try the Spice Route Flagship Syrah.
3. **Sweet potato gnocchi with shredded lamb shank (p 96), followed by ginger, cranberry and almond semifreddo (p 166)**

A red blend is in order here, where the tannins will be softened by the richness of the dish. Try out the Rustenberg John X Merriman.

4. **Spicy gruyère-crusted fishcakes (p 125) with honey-roasted sweet potatoes (p 143) and grilled pear and goat's cheese salad (p 55), followed by granadilla cheesecake in a glass (p 162)**
   The honeyed, yet subtle nature of this dish allows for the pairing of a delicate Chenin Blanc. I would recommend the Raats Original Chenin Blanc.
5. **Chicken butternut and feta pie (p 83) followed by crispy ginger, pear and apple tart (p 155).**
   A full-flavoured Chardonnay please! Treat yourself to the Jordan Nine Yards Chardonnay.
6. **Parma ham and melon salad (p 61), followed by baked risotto (p 141) and then pears poached in red wine with vanilla mascarpone (p 165)**
   This needs a wine with smoke and a small slice of butter, so the Ataraxia Chardonnay comes to mind.
7. **Roast pork belly (p 115) served with polenta with roasted butternut and crispy sage (p 145), followed by white chocolate and berry mille-feuille (p 161)**
   This is a very versatile dish to pair with wine, but give it a bash with a good Merlot. A superb option is the Bein Merlot, the smallest producer in South Africa.
8. **Grilled soy and honey salmon (p 119) served with lemony asparagus and boiled baby potatoes, followed by mini pavlovas with white chocolate mousse and berry coulis (p 157)**
   This dish requires the flavour profile of a Sauvignon Blanc with the mouth feel of a Chardonnay, so the best bet is a delicious Bordeaux-style white blend. Try the Oak Valley OV blend of Sauvignon Blanc and Sémillon.

RECIPE INDEX.

Page numbers in **bold** type indicate photographs